kaukasis

kaukasis

a culinary journey through
Georgia, Azerbaijan & beyond

OLIA HERCULES

weldon**owen**

weldon**owen**

Published in North America by Weldon Owen, Inc.
1045 Sansome Street, Suite 100, San Francisco, CA 94111
www.weldonowen.com
Weldon Owen is a division of Bonnier Publishing USA

First published in Great Britain in 2017 by
Mitchell Beazley, a division of
Octopus Publishing Group Ltd

ISBN: 978-1-68188-303-8

Library of Congress Cataloging-in-Publication data is available

Printed and bound in China

This edition printed in 2017
10 9 8 7 6 5 4 3 2 1

Photographer Elena Heatherwick
Cover Designer Grace Helmer
Food Stylist Olia Hercules

To the people of the Caucasus –
the most charismatic people in the world

Contents

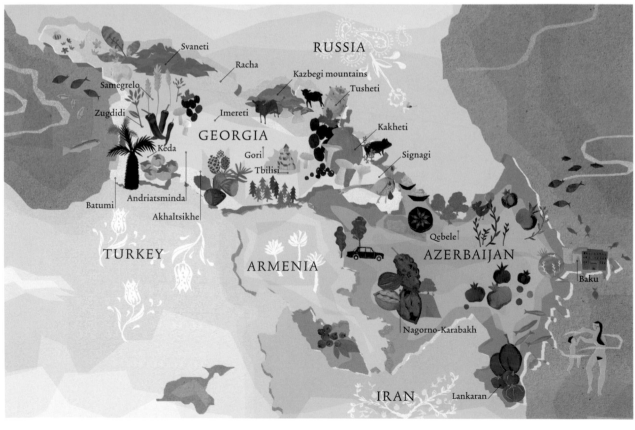

Introduction

Finding the name for this book was one of the hardest things I have ever had to do. How does one unite the idea of a childhood journey, memories, and feelings of nostalgia with newfound knowledge of the Caucasus and its people? These folks may share the same geographical region, culture, and much of their cooking, but they don't necessarily revere each other, or at least they often say they don't for various complicated reasons.

In the light of recent and not-so-recent events, where more and more neighboring countries have gone to war and lost connections that have been cemented for centuries or have foolishly erected further barriers between them, I slipped into even more of a pitfall trying to navigate my way around and write sensitively about my family and friends' lifelong experiences.

In times of great economic struggle, people fall apart. I have seen it happen on a personal level, where close friends, parents and their children, or siblings break ties with each other because it is simply very hard. When it's hard to survive financially, hard to stay strong together, and hard to make sense of history and events, it's easy to forget what unites us.

On a greater scale, the same happens with entire countries, which fall out and drag us even further along the road of alienation and conflict, inciting hatred, misunderstandings, and worse. This happened to my Armenian family, who are originally from Nagorno-Karabakh and have inspired me to write this book.

A war broke out in Karabakh in the 1980s, forcing them first to abandon their summer house and then to leave that region and eventually Azerbaijan's capital Baku to relocate to Kiev, the capital of Ukraine. Their house was largely destroyed, with only their huge beloved library room still standing with hundreds of books left abandoned and rotting on the shelves. Yet despite the anguish, mutual hostility, and atrocities, I have not once heard my Armenian aunt say anything negative about Azerbaijanis. She has always reiterated that it was an artificially created conflict, like so many of them were at the time – and still are.

I was taught from the start (perhaps in rather naive terms, but...) that people and human values are universal. Whether you are Armenian, Azerbaijani, or Georgian, or one of any of the smaller Caucasian peoples, so much of the culture of the region is intertwined and destinies interwoven, and – on a more domestic level – so many cooking techniques and dishes are shared and borrowed. Geopolitics can often be an ugly, unfortunate reality, just like unemployment, financial difficulties, and any of those other man-made afflictions. But I am glad that I grew up without having to take any sides. We cherished our Armenian, Azeri, Georgian, Ossetian, Karachai, and Adegei friends all the same, equally interested in what they had to say, what they remembered, what they held dear and, of course, what they cooked!

In seeking my book title, words kept running through my head: *Caucasus, togetherness, communion, "as one," family, table, polyphony, layers, together.* One word, I needed just one word to unite us all, but not in a tragic, forceful way like the word "Soviet" once did. I needed one word to unite our complicated histories, our families' memories, our new experiences in the most peaceful and natural way.

I tried a couple of options that I felt very strongly about, both powerful Georgian words, but sadly they didn't gel. In desperation, and following my best friend's wise counsel, I wrote a couple of pages on why I decided to write this book – a messy "stream of consciousness" kind of essay. And when I finished, I realized that I was overcomplicating things. The name doesn't have to be too clever, enigmatic, or esoteric. The place itself, Caucasus, is mysterious enough.

Being an avid fan of etymology, I recalled reading that the name "Caucasus" possibly originated from the Scythian language (the Scythians being an ancient civilization from the Ukrainian steppe where I was born) and is akin to the gorgeous Greek word *Kaukasis*. It means "snowy mountain top" – and at that moment the title of the book was born! At the very top of the Kazbegi mountains in northeastern Georgia, I saw a viewing platform with a massive mosaic. It was beautiful. What I loved the most was that the animals and people depicted have clearly defined outlines, but within these outlines their forms are made up of mismatched colored tiles. This is how I feel about culture, and about traditions and recipes. The outlines are there, set in stone, but what's happening inside is a big puzzle of individual fragments, multicolored and seemingly mismatched.

I hope you also approach this book as such. Get inspired by the outlines, but also feel compelled to create your own mosaic. This is my interpretation, a symbol, a vision of how to cherish tradition while also being open to creating something new.

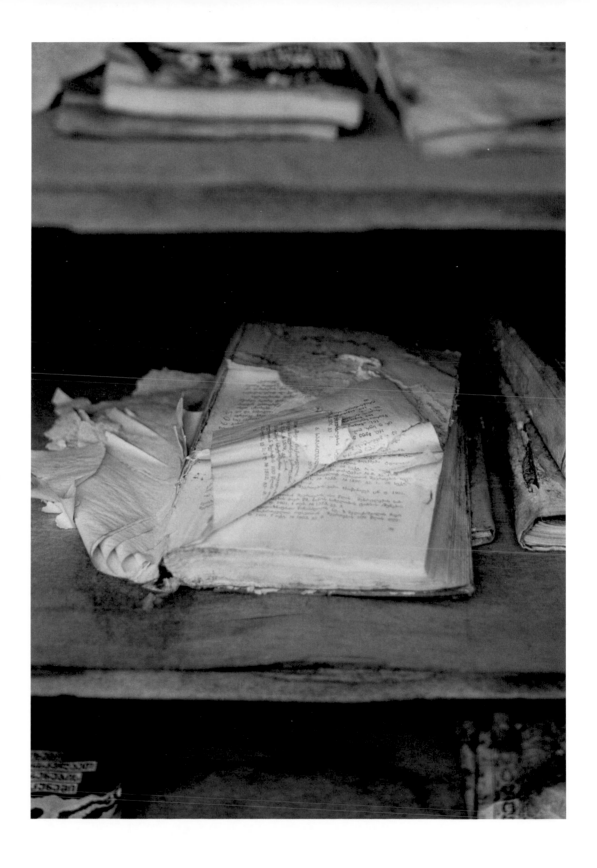

"I like vegetables, especially in spring," declared our Georgian guide, Shota. Such a simple thing to say, but it rang so true and got stuck in my head. It had so much meaning. In our modern world we can get tomatoes, cucumbers, and herbs all year round. Of course, nowadays you can too in the Caucasus, but people still tend to eat seasonally. The first fresh vegetables of spring, the first herbs, the first sweet prickly cucumber – these ingredients are never better to enjoy than immediately after the long winter months.

roots, shoots, leaves & all

12   roots, shoots, leaves & all

Beets & plums

The combination of beets and plums was such a revelation to me that I immediately set about creating different versions of the authentic Georgian way of marinating beet in the tart plum sauce called *tkemali*. I couldn't choose which was the best, so I am giving two versions of the salad: the traditional approach, and a roasted version for when plums are readily available but you can't be bothered to make the sauce. The roasted version will give you a taste similar to the original with the added pleasure of biting into caramelized plums and bitter leaves that contribute texture and a welcome savoriness. I use small, tart Alycha plums here, but slightly underripe greengages or ordinary plums also work very well.

The original charkhali, or plum-marinated beet

This is a method for making beet *charkhali* the authentic way, which is simple and delicious. But if you are short of time, you don't have to marinate it overnight – you can serve the beets in the *tkemali* immediately. It's brilliant, though, because if you have any left over, you can store it in the refrigerator and it will start to pickle. It should keep for up to a week if fully covered by the sauce. Serve with a splash of date molasses or honey if it seems too tart.

Serves 8 as a side

4½ lb (2 kg) beets, scrubbed really well

1 tablespoon sea salt flakes

2 cups (18 oz/500 g) Tina's Fresh Tkemali (page 23), unsweetened

Bring 2 qt (64 fl oz/2 L) water to a boil in a saucepan, add the unpeeled beets, and season with the salt. Cook until the beets are easily pierced with a knife but still al dente, 30–40 minutes.

Drain the beets and leave until cool enough to handle, then peel and cut them into wedges.

Pop the beets into a bowl, pour the *tkemali* over, and leave to marinate overnight in the refrigerator before serving.

VARIATION
Try roasting the same quantity of peeled beet wedges in a roasting pan in a preheated oven at 350°F (180°C), until soft and starting to caramelize at the edges, about 30–40 minutes. Add the *tkemali*, covering the beets with it, and roast for a further 5–10 minutes. Then serve with a handful of chopped cilantro and some thinly sliced green onions.

Beets, plums & bitter leaves

Serves 4–6

2 tablespoons canola or mild olive oil

1 lb (500 g) beets, peeled and quartered

5 plums, pitted and quartered

1 tablespoon red wine vinegar

sea salt flakes

5 oz (150 g) Treviso (or ordinary) radicchio

1 red chile, with seeds, sliced

2 teaspoons maple syrup or honey

2 garlic cloves, crushed

2 teaspoons sesame seeds, toasted

a handful of soft herbs, chopped – dill and cilantro work really well here (optional)

Preheat the oven to 400°F (200°C).

Add the oil to a roasting pan and heat it in the oven for 5 minutes.

Add the beets, plums, and vinegar to the roasting pan, season with salt, and roast for 30 minutes.

Leaving a little of the stalk in place, slice the radicchio into thin wedges. Add it to the beet pan with the chile, maple syrup, and a bit more salt, and give it all a good stir. Roast for a further 10 minutes.

Add the garlic and stir it through the contents of the pan, then remove the pan from the oven.

Sprinkle with the sesame seeds and herbs (if using) and serve.

VARIATIONS

You can use any bitter crunchy vegetable instead of radicchio. Belgian endive would work well, as would sliced cultivated dandelion greens. Any toasted seed or nut can be substituted for sesame. I have also tried this with blackberries and black currants instead of plums and it worked wonders – beet loves any dark, rich fruit that has a little acidity. I sometimes like to serve this with watercress or arugula.

Ia's salad

I love simple but unusual salads, when one tiny ingredient turns something so familiar into an incredible dish that you can't get enough of. This happened when I tasted Tomer Amedi's (head chef of The Palomar restaurant) mum's Yemeni tomato salad with green chiles and chopped lemon with its skin still on. And this happened again when I went to Megrelia (or Samegrelo, as Georgians call it) in western Georgia and met Ia, a school head teacher with a penchant for etymology, thin cigarettes, and coffee. A modest addition of seasoned *adjika* salt makes this salad so piquant and "moreish." I also love how the spring onions and herbs are cut into large chunks, almost treated like a vegetable rather than a mere seasoning.

Serves 2–4

DRESSING

3 tablespoons white wine vinegar

1 teaspoon Red Adjika Salt (page 62) or pinch of cayenne pepper

sea salt flakes, to taste (if using cayenne)

pinch of superfine sugar or honey to taste (optional)

1 head of escarole or romaine or similar lettuce, cut into large chunks

1 bunch of spring onions or green onions, sliced into ½-inch (1-cm) chunks

¼ red onion, sliced (optional)

½ bunch of cilantro, stalks and all, roughly chopped

½ bunch of flat-leaf parsley, stalks and all, roughly chopped

½ cucumber, thinly sliced

2 ripe tomatoes, chopped (optional)

For the dressing, mix the vinegar and *adjika* salt and sea salt together. Taste and add a little sugar if you think it needs it (I often do add sugar or honey here).

Mix the rest of the ingredients together in a large bowl, then pour the dressing over and gently combine with your fingers – Ia insisted I mix it as if I were touching feathers.

Tips *I would add the red onion if this salad is to be served with barbecued meats; otherwise, leave it out for a much more delicate result. If you can't be bothered to make the adjika and can't find it ready-prepared, don't worry; this salad will be lovely with a simple lemon, salt, and honey dressing spiked with some smoked paprika or a little cayenne.*

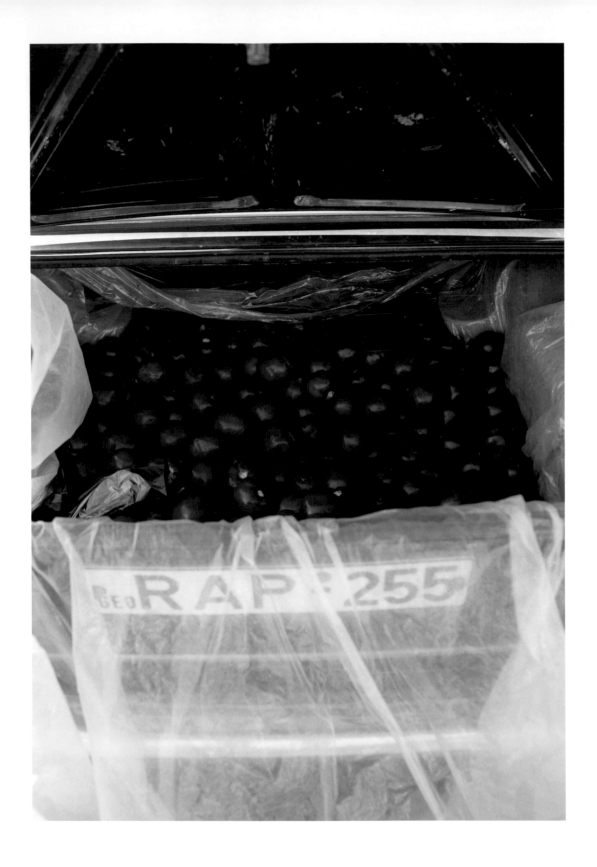

Satsebeli

Nobody makes small quantities of *satsebeli* in Samegrelo, western Georgia. They would normally use about a hundred pounds of tomatoes to bottle enough to last all winter. And no wonder, as this is an amazing sauce. It's good with roast chicken, it's incredible drizzled over eggs or polenta, and it's also the bomb when drizzled inside a juicy lamb burger or served with refried *khinkali* dumplings (see page 85). The original recipe would have required you to buy a special oar and cistern for stirring and cooking this sauce, but I have scaled down the quantities for non-Georgian home use.

Makes about 2 cups (16 fl oz/ 500 ml)
  2¾ lb (1.25 kg) tomatoes, chopped
  sea salt flakes, to taste
  8 oz (250 g) red bell peppers, cored, seeded and chopped
  7 garlic cloves, chopped

1¾ oz (50 g) Red Adjika Salt (page 62) or 4 teaspoons sea salt with a pinch of cayenne pepper
sunflower oil, to cover (if storing)

If storing longer term, you will also need enough sterilized airtight bottles or jars to hold 2 qt (2 L) in total

Put the chopped tomatoes in a bowl with a handful of sea salt flakes, cover, and leave overnight to release their juices if you have time. If not, blitz them in a blender or food processor.

Transfer the tomatoes to a saucepan, add the bell peppers, and cook slowly over low heat until the peppers are soft and the tomatoes have reduced to a third of their original volume, 40–60 minutes. Leave to cool a little, then blitz in the blender or food processor and pass through a sieve.

Put the mixture back into the cleaned pan, add the garlic and *adjika*, and cook for a further 30 minutes, stirring from time to time to mix in the *adjika* and avoid a crust forming on top. Taste, and if needed season with salt – this sauce should be ever so slightly saltier than you think it needs to be if you want it to keep for a long time. But if you are planning to eat it within a week, season with as much salt as you feel comfortable with, then leave to cool and store in an airtight container in the refrigerator.

If storing over the winter, transfer the cooled sauce to sterilized airtight bottles or jars and pour a thin film of oil on top to help it keep for longer. Seal and store in a cool, dark place.

Kohlrabi, sorrel, radish & endive salad with tkemali dressing

I love taking inspiration from ingredients that I encounter on my travels and using them in ways that they wouldn't necessarily be used in their home country. *Tkemali*, the ubiquitous Georgian plum and wild mint condiment, is traditionally eaten with everything – meat, fish, eggs – but apart from beets (see page 13), not so much with vegetables. Its qualities, however, are those of a really superior dressing – tart, a little spicy, and garlicky with a hint of sweetness – and it works so well with bitter crunchy vegetables. Do experiment with the ingredients here; I bet it would work equally well with some young sweet cabbage, robust lettuce, or radicchio.

Serves 4
   1 tablespoon pomegranate molasses
   ¼ cup (1¾ oz/50 g) Tina's Fresh Tkemali (page 23)
   sea salt flakes
   honey to taste (optional)
   2 heads Belgian endive, sliced lengthwise into 8 wedges
   1 kohlrabi, peeled and thinly sliced
   2 oz (50 g) radishes, thinly sliced
   1 oz (25 g) sorrel leaves or watercress

For the dressing, mix the molasses through the *tkemali*, then taste, adding some salt or a little honey if you think it's too tart. It should really taste strong and pack a punch.

Toss the endive, kohlrabi, and radishes in a bowl, then arrange in a serving dish with the sorrel leaves and serve with the dressing drizzled over.

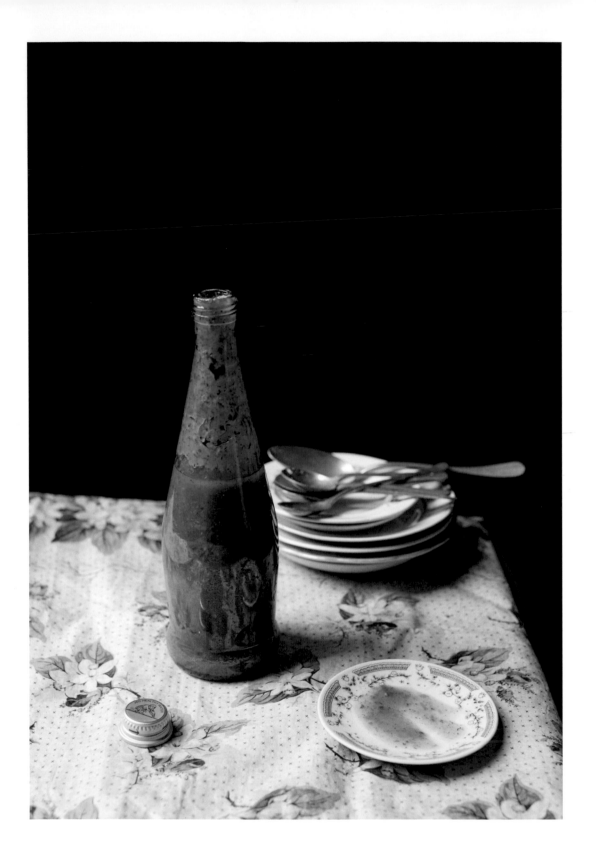

roots, shoots, leaves & all

Tina's fresh tkemali

Tkemali is one of the cornerstones of Georgian cooking. There are as many variations as there are households. Normally the formula involves cooking the tiny Alycha or *tkemali* plums until they can be passed through a sieve, getting rid of the pits and skin and leaving you with the most wonderful plum pulp. Then it is cooked down with garlic and other flavorings like dill. Tina, a village doctor, farmer, and the gentlest soul, who lives high up in the mountains of Svaneti in the northwest, makes this version where the plums are hardly cooked. She prefers it fresh, she says, and I love her style. This recipe is perfect for cooking with or for dressing beets (see page 13).

Makes 1 qt (1.2 L) if not cooked down too much
- 3¼ lb (1.5 kg) yellow and red Alycha plums (or greengages or ordinary plums)
- ½ tablespoon ground *ombalo* (pennyroyal) or dried mint
- ½ tablespoon dill seeds or ½ teaspoon fennel seeds
- 1 teaspoon ground coriander
- 1 teaspoon ground blue fenugreek
- 5 garlic cloves, grated
- ½ teaspoon cayenne pepper
- sea salt flakes and freshly ground black pepper

You will also need four 10–fl oz (300-ml) sterilized preserving jars

Put your yellow and red plums (or whatever plums you have managed to procure) whole into a saucepan. Add a splash of water and let them come up to a boil. Cook until they become soft and separate easily from their pits, about 10 minutes.

Leave the plums until cool enough to handle, then remove the skins and pits. If a little bit of skin remains, it's not a big deal.

Mix the plum flesh with the rest of the ingredients, season to taste, and cook for a further 2 minutes.

While the sauce is still hot, transfer it to the sterilized jars, seal the jars, and immerse them in a deep saucepan of simmering water for a few minutes. Then seal and store in a cool, dark place all winter or, if eating straight away, keep in the refrigerator.

Tip Although I love this version, sometimes the sauce turns out just too astringent (which it's supposed to be authentically), so I add a large tablespoon of muscovado sugar or blackstrap molasses and cook it down for a further 10 minutes rather than 2 minutes. The resulting version has more body to it and is a little deeper in flavor – more like chutney.

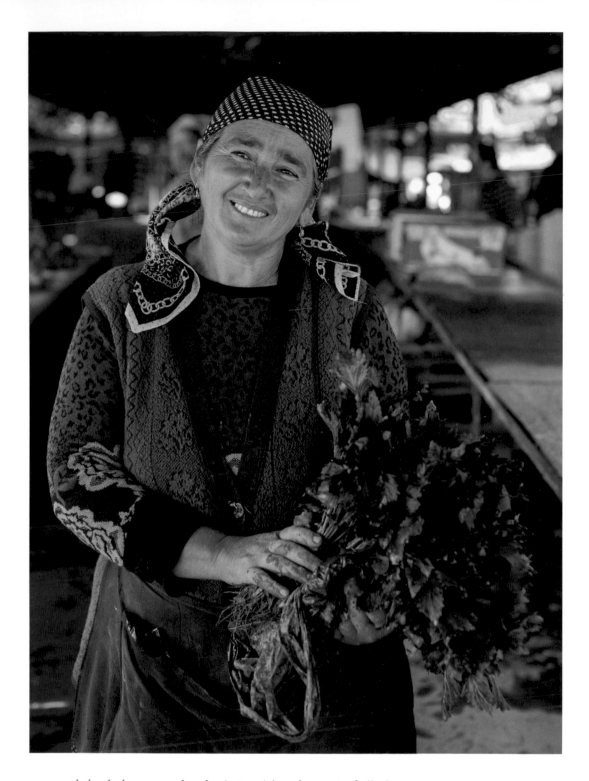

The best herb growers and vendors in Georgia's markets are Azerbaijani women.
Georgians lovingly call them badji (sister) in Azerbaijani.

Mint adjika

This is my favorite paste of all time. It is so easy to make, keeps for months, and is incredibly versatile. A lot of women in western Georgia have a jar of this in their refrigerator. They mix it through stretchy cheese when they make their national western Georgian dish called *elardji*, and it does indeed go so well with creamy fresh cheeses, such as in the Fruit, Mint Adjika & Dairy toast recipe on page 26. Brush a smidgen on some sourdough toast topped with good mozzarella. Alternatively, stir it through boiled new potatoes.

Makes about 1⅔ cups (13 fl oz/375 ml)

4½ oz (125 g) spearmint or ordinary mint, stalks and all

10 green chiles, half seeded

5 garlic cloves

3½ teaspoons (¾ oz/20 g) sea salt flakes

Blitz everything together in a powerful blender or food processor to a paste, or bash it lovingly using a mortar and pestle if you want to feel like an authentic Georgian *bebia* (grandma).

This is a wet flavored salt, so use sparingly. Store in the fridge for up to 1 month.

Green adjika

There are as many *adjika* recipes as there are *tkemali* (plum sauce) recipes, and every woman has her own. I love this one that I picked up in the city of Zugdidi in the western Georgian province of Samegrelo. Stir a little bit through plain cooked legumes or through yogurt. It is also excellent used as a base for a dressing for roast root vegetables, or with added gherkins or capers over soft-boiled eggs.

Makes about 1⅔ cups (13 fl oz/400 ml)

2 celery ribs, roughly chopped

1 bunch of cilantro, leaves, stalks and well-washed roots (if the roots are available)

1 bunch of flat-leaf parsley, stalks and all

1 bunch of basil, stalks only

5 garlic cloves, roughly chopped

10 green chiles (leave the seeds in if you like it hotter)

3½ teaspoons (¾ oz/20 g) sea salt flakes

Blitz everything together in a powerful blender or food processor. You will end up with a wet, green paste.

Store in the refrigerator for up to 1 month.

Fruit, mint adjika & dairy

Georgia is a country that manages to completely mess with your head. Had I not had my son, I probably would have moved there at the first opportunity. Truth be told, I actually considered moving even with my toddler son. But when I was back in London, the trance I was in lifted and I came to my senses. This didn't happen to Ének Peterson, a young American who decided to take a short trip around Georgia but stayed on and is now cooking tasty, creative dishes in Vino Underground, a natural-wine bar in Tbilisi. This is my version of a bruschetta she served me. It is one of the best combinations around. Sweet fruit, tangy cheese, spicy and fresh mint paste – nothing short of genius. Any seasonal fruit will work, such as persimmon, pears, or apples in winter, or nectarines or apricots in summer. My Italian friends now say it's their favorite "bruschetta." I hope they won't be alone. Eat as a casual snack or make loads of little ones and feed a party.

Serves 5 as a snack
   5 thin slices of sourdough bread
   1 tablespoon Mint Adjika (page 25)
   2 oz (50 g) mild goat cheese or labneh
   2 firm apricots, pitted and sliced, or 1 persimmon, thinly sliced
   mint leaves, to garnish

Toast the bread, then brush with the mint *adjika* – be careful, as it's really salty and should be used sparingly, as a seasoning.

Top with the goat cheese and your choice of fruit, and sprinkle over some mint.

Homemade matsoni

To make this recipe (a type of yogurt made with the special Caspian bacteria), the likes of which you've never tasted before, you first need a *matsoni* starter. When I was writing this book in Svaneti, northwest Georgia, my brain was so overtaken by it all that I had a dream that I was by the shore of the Caspian Sea scraping ancient fossils with a spoon, "collecting" this bacteria. Surreal romantic visions aside, you can find this online. Or go to a Georgian restaurant and ask them for some *deda* or a little *matsoni* in a plastic bottle. I've known people who have made contact with Georgians in their area on Instagram – the community is so friendly and welcoming, I am sure someone will be willing to help you. Failing all else, contact me and I'll give you some. A handful is all you need to begin creating something incredibly wonderful, healthy and, most importantly to me, tasty. It has so many uses in this book, and I am sure you will find new creative uses for it, too.

Makes about 2 qt (2 L)
  1 qt (½ gallon/2.1 L) raw milk
  1 heaping tablespoon *matsoni* or raw milk yogurt
  (available from well-stocked farmers' markets)

  You will also need a warm blanket or large towel

Heat the milk in a saucepan until it just "bites" your finger. Whisk the *matsoni* through the milk and immediately remove from the heat. Cover the pan with a lid, then wrap the pan in a warm blanket or large towel. Place somewhere warm for 24 hours. Do not move or disturb the pan, just leave it to sit.

The next day, the mixture should look like a thick yogurt, but this will depend on how fatty the milk you used was. You may have to leave it for a few hours longer.

In the Caucasus, some people make a fresh batch of the yogurt every day, and it is best used within 24 hours or so – otherwise, it will become too sour. But any leftovers can be stored in the coldest part of the refrigerator and will be pleasant to eat for up to 4 days. It can be kept for longer (2 weeks) but will turn sour and will only be good used as a starter. If the milk has turned funky and smells of alcohol, it is best not used for anything.

Zucchini & garlic matsoni

This dish is simplicity itself. It used to be made with mayonnaise throughout the ex–Soviet Union, but thank goodness that's all over and we can now use traditional premium dairy. As with all simple recipes, this is particularly tasty if you can source great homegrown or good-quality zucchini and make your own *matsoni*. If your zucchini are not the greatest, try using a mixture of all the soft herbs you like best to give them a bit of a lift. But if you have amazing vegetables and your own homemade yogurt, use just a little dill and let them sing their sweet, gentle song. And I love borage for its subtle cucumber flavor overtones.

Serves 4 as a side
  2 large zucchini
  4 tablespoons vegetable oil
  6 tablespoons (3½ oz/100 g) Homemade Matsoni (page 29) or good-quality plain yogurt
  2 garlic cloves, crushed
  sea salt flakes
  1 tablespoon of your favorite mixture of soft herbs, roughly chopped

Slice the zucchini lengthwise into ¼-inch (5-mm) strips.

Heat the oil in a large frying pan and fry the zucchini slices on each side over medium heat until deep golden. Remove and drain them on paper towels.

Mix the *matsoni* with the garlic and add some salt, then taste – it should be really well seasoned, so add more salt if necessary. Drizzle the mixture over the zucchini and sprinkle with the herbs.

VARIATION
Try lightly coating the zucchini in flour before frying – it will give them a bit more body. Buckwheat flour adds a nice nuttiness to the flavor.

Chestnut plov with squash & walnut crust

I happened to meet a film crew of old recipe hunters in Azerbaijan, a group of five men who traveled all around the country seeking out forgotten recipes for their TV show. My brother and I got lucky and went along. We climbed through freezing mountain springs and off-roaded until we reached a village where the most gorgeous woman cooked us a *plov* and told us about her life. She also told me about this *plov*, with its most unusual *gazmakh*, or crust. You can serve this with meat, but to me the chestnuts and plump dried fruit do the job. Since dried fruit is one of the main ingredients, try to find good-quality fruits with no added sulfites.

Serves 6

1¾ cups (12 oz/350 g) basmati rice

9 oz (250 g) Delicata squash or other good winter squash, peeled, seeded, and grated

1 cup (3½ oz/100 g) walnuts, ground into a paste with a powerful blender or with a mortar and pestle

fine sea salt

⅔ cup (5½ oz/150 g) Clarified Butter (page 53)

pinch of saffron threads

small pinch of rock salt

7 oz (200 g) peeled chestnuts, roasted and roughly chopped, or vacuum-packed

½ cup (2¼ oz/60 g) dried apricots, sliced

⅓ cup (2¼ oz/60 g) raisins

First, wash the rice well in several changes of cold water to get rid of as much starch as possible. Then cook it in a large saucepan in plenty of well-salted boiling water until it is almost cooked, about 7 minutes. Drain it well and spread it on a sheet pan to let off a bit of the steam.

Mix the grated squash with the walnut paste and a pinch of fine sea salt, combining the ingredients thoroughly (the moisture from the squash and the walnut oils should help it stick together). Taste and add more salt if you think you need it.

Heat 3 tablespoons of the clarified butter in a 9-inch (23-cm) diameter heavy-bottomed saucepan, then spread the squash and nut paste all over the base of the pan in a thin layer and cook over medium heat for 1–2 minutes. Reduce the heat to the lowest-possible setting and add the rice, in batches, making sure that it falls in loosely – try not to pack it down. Cover the pan with a kitchen towel and then cover with a lid and cook for 30 minutes.

Meanwhile, melt 6 tablespoons (2½ oz/ 70 g) of the clarified butter in a pan. Using a mortar and pestle, grind the saffron with the rock salt, then scrape it into the melted butter. Set aside to infuse.

*Salim and Halima Akhmadov (center), surrounded
by three generations of their family.*

Once the rice has been cooking for 30 minutes, lift the lid and kitchen towel, then make holes in the rice with the handle of a wooden spoon and pour the saffron butter all over. Remove from the heat and leave, covered, while you prepare the nuts and dried fruit.

Heat the remaining clarified butter in a large frying pan over low heat and cook the chestnuts, dried fruit, and a sprinkling of salt until they look plump and are warmed through, about 5–7 minutes.

When the rice is *dan dan* – the Azerbaijani term for fluffy, perky, perfectly cooked rice – take it out of the pan gently and put into a beautiful serving dish. Now check your squash crust – it should be nicely caramelized, not burnt, and if that's the case, gently scrape it off the base of the pan and sprinkle over the rice. Add the buttery chestnuts and dried fruit on top, and serve alongside some sharp salads, whole bunches of herbs, and grilled meat or vegetables.

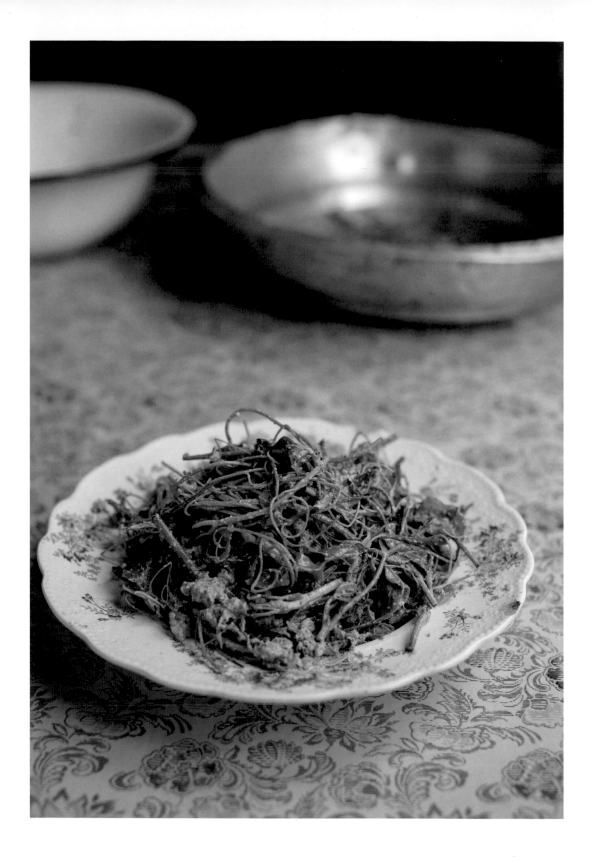

Ekala pkhali

Ekala is a wild plant found in Georgia that resembles young vine shoots and has a mildly sour and pleasantly musky flavor. I love finding an ingredient as exotic as this at a market – it fills me with awe and a sense of wonder. Can you imagine seeing wild foraged food on sale at your local market like it was the norm?! I doubt you will be able to find ekala outside of Georgia, but the walnut paste works perfectly well with any one of the other blanched leaves suggested.

Serves 2

  10 oz (300 g) *ekala* or purslane, Swiss chard, beet greens, or spinach

  2 small garlic cloves, peeled

  sea salt flakes

  ¼ teaspoon cayenne pepper

  ½ teaspoon dried blue fenugreek

  1½ cups (5½ oz/150 g) walnuts

  2 tablespoons white wine vinegar or lemon juice

  1 teaspoon honey, or to taste

Bring a saucepan of salted water to a boil and dip in your greens of choice to blanch – *ekala* and purslane need 30 seconds before immediately draining and refreshing under cold running water, Swiss chard stalks 2 minutes, Swiss chard leaves and beet greens a minute, and with spinach I would just dip it in and out of the boiling water. As soon as the greens have cooled down in the cold water, drain them well.

To make the *pkhali* paste, bash the garlic cloves with some sea salt flakes in a mortar with a pestle. Then add the cayenne, fenugreek, and walnuts, and keep grinding until the mixture starts to resemble a paste. Add the vinegar and honey to the paste and taste it, adding a little more salt or sweetness to your taste.

Toss the drained greens in the walnut paste and serve with bread for a light lunch or as part of a bigger feast.

VARIATION
Georgians also slightly overcook runner beans and then muddle them with the pestle alongside the paste in the mortar. In the West, we have been taught that overcooking beans is a mistake, and it usually is, but in combination with this fragrant paste, the "overcooked" runner beans provide flavor and comfort. Try it.

Badrijani nigvzit or eggplant rolls

There are so many recipes for stuffed eggplants in the Caucasus – some simple, some more complicated. I tasted this in my beloved city of Zugdidi (western Georgia) and this is just how I have been taught to make it. It is one of those perfect universal recipes that will shine all over the world and is now my number one choice if I ever have to cater to a vegetarian friend. It is as filling as it is delectable.

Serves 4

6 tablespoons sunflower oil

2 large eggplants, halved lengthwise

2 onions, diced

1 cup (3½ oz/100 g) walnuts

1 garlic clove, crushed

1 small bunch of flat-leaf parsley, leaves picked and finely chopped

1 small bunch of cilantro, stalks and all, finely chopped

½ teaspoon Red Adjika Salt (page 62) or some cayenne pepper

½ teaspoon Green Adjika (page 25) (optional)

seeds of 1 small pomegranate

sea salt flakes, if needed

Heat ¼ cup of the oil in a large frying pan, add the eggplant halves cut side down, and allow to color. Flip them, then reduce the heat and cover the pan with a lid. The eggplant slices need to be cooked through, soft and malleable, so it may take up to 20 minutes for this to happen – be patient. If you prefer, brush the eggplant halves with the oil, sit them cut side up on a baking sheet, and roast in a preheated 400°F (200°C) oven until nice and golden, 15–20 minutes, then flip and cook until the eggplants seem soft enough to be folded in two, 15 minutes more.

While the eggplants are cooking, make the stuffing. In a frying pan, fry the onions over medium heat in the remaining 2 tablespoons oil until golden, then leave to cool and strain off any excess oil.

Meanwhile, blitz the walnuts until really finely ground in an electric spice or coffee grinder.

Mix together the ground walnuts, cooled strained onions, garlic, herbs, and both *adjikas*, if using, really well. Taste and add salt if needed, then gently stir through half the pomegranate seeds.

Drain the eggplant halves on paper towels. Spread a tablespoon of the stuffing along each eggplant half, then fold in two. Place a tiny bit of the stuffing on top and add a few more pomegranate seeds to garnish.

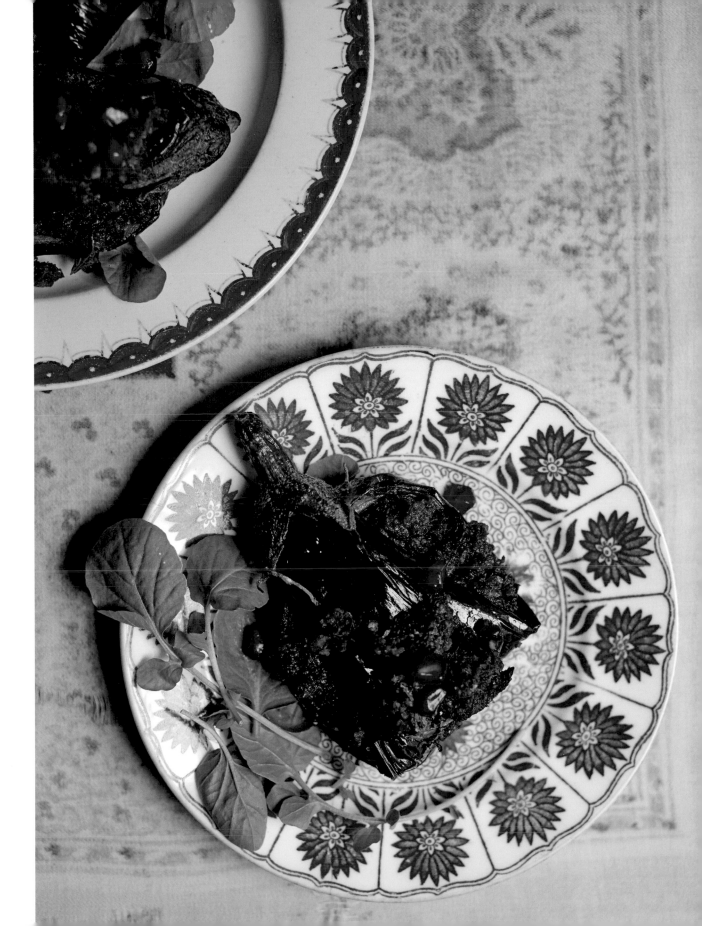

Gia's mushrooms & egg

It was in the town of Signagi in the eastern Georgian region of Kakheti where I tried some of the most delicious and inventive, without being contrived, cooking. "Good food doesn't have to be complicated, overworked," remarked Gia, head chef at an incredibly beautiful restaurant (of natural-wine fame – see page 233) called Pheasant's Tears. And I agree with him wholeheartedly. With a few wonderful ingredients, knowledge of tradition, and a creative mind like Gia's, Georgian cooking is taken to another level. This dish is so simple, but I would award it and the others that we tasted numerous stars and accolades. Just find excellent mushrooms, really good eggs, some aromatics, and a tiny bit of spice, and you have a beauty of a dish.

Serves 2 as a sharing starter

   3 tablespoons unsalted butter

   1 tablespoon olive oil

   2 garlic cloves, sliced

   2 field mushrooms, brushed clean

   7 oz (200 g) wild mushrooms, such as black trumpet
   mushrooms or chanterelles, brushed clean

   1 egg

   1 green chile, thinly sliced (keep the seeds if you like heat)

   a few sprigs of rosemary in winter or tarragon in summer

   sea salt flakes and freshly ground black pepper

Preheat the oven to 350°F (180°C).

Heat the butter and oil in an ovenproof dish in the oven, or in an ovenproof frying pan on the stove top. Add the garlic and let it sizzle for a moment, just enough to release its aroma, then add all the mushrooms and spoon the sizzling fat over to cover them. Cook in the oven for 10 minutes, or cook on the stove top over medium-low heat, shaking from time to time, until the mushrooms have softened, about 5 minutes.

Crack the egg into the middle of the dish or pan and sprinkle with the chile, herbs, and some salt and pepper. Cook in the oven until the whites are set and the yolk is cooked to your liking, 5–10 minutes.

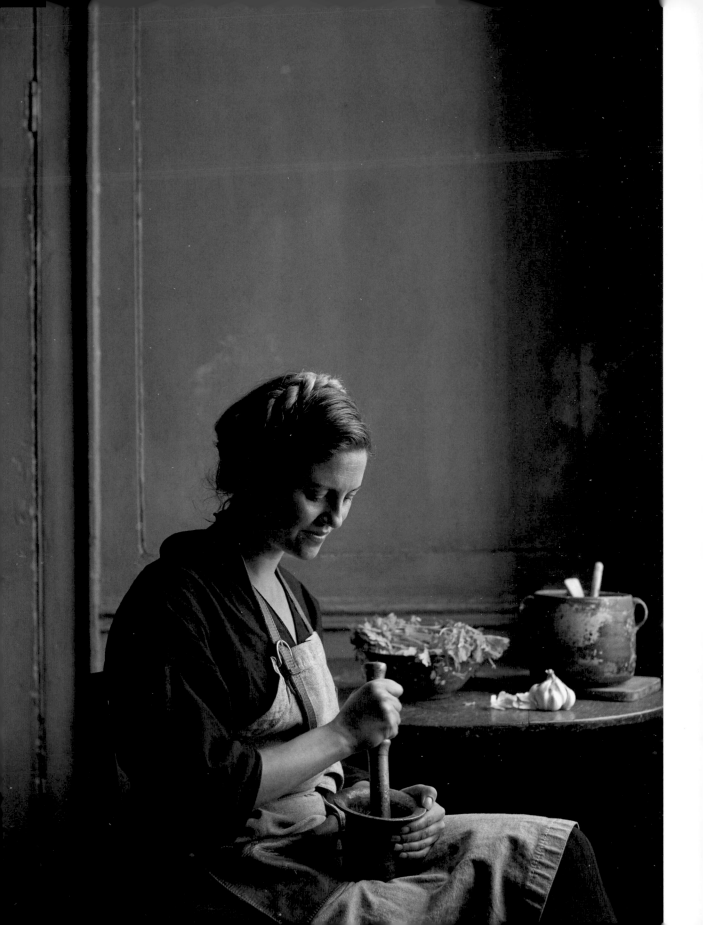

Adjapsandali

"How's life?" "Akh, my life is a total *adjapsandali* at the moment." This is what you may hear a couple of Georgians saying to each other, and it would mean that someone's life is in complete (but delicious) chaos. Here the term is applied to a ratatouille-style assortment of veg, to which you may respond, another ratatouille? But what a version it is. If ratatouille is a humble peasant, then *adjapsandali* is the knight of spring vegetable stews. There is nothing prosaic about this dish. If you are short of time or endearingly lazy, or have homegrown vegetables that are so flavorsome that they don't need any help with taste, skip browning the veg in the pan. Just layer them with the onion and cook in the oven, adding the herb paste and marigold powder or saffron at the very end. Whatever you do, don't skip the last step where you smash a variety of soft herbs with garlic – do it. This is what gives this seemingly modest dish its *cojones*. Saffron is not authentic – Georgians would add what they call "Imereti saffron" or "yellow flower," – marigold flowers dried and ground – and if you can find the good stuff, get it, as it tastes like floral fungi. But if marigold is not available, a tiny bit of saffron adds a certain *je ne sais quoi*.

Serves 4–6

4 tablespoons sunflower oil

2 potatoes, peeled and thinly sliced

1 eggplant, sliced into rounds

1 red bell pepper, cored, seeded and chopped

1 green bell pepper, cored, seeded and chopped

10 runner beans, chopped

1 large onion, thinly sliced

3 garlic cloves, 2 roughly chopped, 1 left whole

1 red chile (seeded if you want less heat), chopped

pinch of powdered dried marigold petals or a tiny pinch of saffron threads (optional)

sea salt flakes and freshly ground black pepper

1 teaspoon dried blue fenugreek (or use ground coriander or ground cumin)

1 bunch of cilantro, leaves, stalks and well-washed roots (if the latter are available)

1 large ripe tomato

handful of roughly chopped purple or green basil

handful of roughly chopped dill

handful of chopped tarragon

small handful of chopped summer savory (if available) or a pinch of dried

warm crusty bread, to serve

continued »

Heat 2 tablespoons of the sunflower oil in a large saucepan over medium-high heat and (if you have the time and are after deep flavors) sauté the potatoes, eggplant, peppers, and beans in batches briskly, adding a little bit more oil as you go if the pan becomes dry. Remove the vegetables to a bowl.

Now add another tablespoon of oil in the pan, reduce the heat to medium-low, add the onion, the 2 chopped garlic cloves, and chile and cook slowly, drawing out the onion's sugars, until it is all meltingly sweet and golden, about 15 minutes. If you prefer a fresher flavor, skip this step and simply add the onion, garlic, and chile as they are to the rest of the veg.

Bash the marigold petals (or saffron) with some salt using a mortar and pestle and add a splash of water. Then add this together with the blue fenugreek (or other warm spices of your choice) to the pan.

Chop the cilantro stalks and roots very finely and layer with the vegetables in the pan.

Cut the tomato in half and grate it. If it's a good tomato, I don't throw away the skin but chop it and use it, too. Add to the vegetables, season well with salt and pepper, and add a splash of water if you think it needs it. Cover with a lid and cook gently for 30 minutes, then uncover and cook over medium heat for a further 5 minutes.

Add the remaining garlic clove to your mortar with a little salt, the cilantro leaves and all the other herbs, and gently grind with the pestle. Just before serving, stir this head-spinning herb paste through the warm vegetables and serve with a huge hunk of warm crusty bread.

Tip Don't stress about what soft herbs you can find – this is not a rigid formula. Use whatever soft, fresh aromatics you can procure, including basil, cilantro, tarragon, dill, chervil, and marjoram, but keep away from sage. Mix and match them together with some salt and garlic, and you will transform a simple ratatouille into the delicious chaos that is our lives and . . . adjapsandali!

Cauliflower steak gratin

Aunt Nina really loves her cauliflower, and she is not shy to get creative with it. She actually uses processed "burger" cheese here and I still enjoy the dish (this may be the only "guilty"pleasure I will ever have), but I think using a good-quality melty cheese is preferable.

Serves 4 as a side
  1 head of cauliflower
  1 tablespoon unsalted butter
  1 tablespoon vegetable oil, plus extra if using the onion
  1 onion, thinly sliced (optional)
  4 eggs, lightly beaten
  2 small garlic cloves, finely grated
  5 oz (150 g) raclette or Ogleshield cheese, grated
  sea salt flakes and freshly ground black pepper
  1 tablespoon chopped cilantro
  1 tablespoon chopped dill

Preheat the oven to 350°F (180°C).

Slice the cauliflower, including the stalks and leaves (if they aren't too nasty), into steaks 1¼ inches (3 cm) thick. Some florets will break away, but keep those as well.

Heat the butter and oil in a large frying pan over medium-high heat, and when really hot, brown the cauliflower steaks on each side. Transfer to a gratin dish.

If using the onion, add some more oil to the frying pan, add the onion slices, and cook gently until soft and golden. This will take 10 minutes or a bit longer, so if you can't be bothered, leave this step out.

Mix the eggs, garlic, cooked onion, if using, and cheese together, and season with salt and pepper. Pour over the cauliflower and bake until the eggs are set and golden, 15–20 minutes. Scatter with the chopped herbs before serving with a fresh green salad.

Gia's polyphony zucchini

I would never in a million years think to pair zucchini and berries, but the dish that Gia made for us at his restaurant, Pheasant's Tears, in Signagi, in the eastern region of Kakheti, was one of the best I have ever eaten. Just like a Georgian polyphonic song that may sound like dissonance to those who are used to the jolly simplicity of pop songs, it was as multilayered as the colors and flavors of a Georgian landscape. All the ingredients were outstanding and sang their own notes, but also came together to create a unique whole.

Serves 4 as a side
  4 tablespoons sunflower oil
  4 shallots or small onions, halved
  2 zucchini, cut into ¾-inch (2-cm) rounds
  5 garlic cloves, cut in half vertically
  2 long green chiles, bruised but left whole
  sea salt flakes and freshly ground black pepper
  handful of fresh sour cherries and/or red currants

Heat the oil in a large frying pan over medium-low heat, add the shallots and cook until they soften and start turning golden. Remove from the pan.

Add the zucchini rounds and brown on each side.

Reduce the heat, add the garlic and chiles, and season everything really well. Cook for 3 minutes.

At the very end, add the sour cherries and/or red currants and switch off the heat. Taste again and season with some extra salt and pepper if it needs it. Serve with sourdough bread or as part of a bigger feast.

Nutty tomato & cucumber salad

Tomatoes and cucumber are another of those standard combinations, but add some nuts, chiles, and an interesting mix of herbs, and you have a different beast altogether. Traditionally, Georgians would of course use walnuts, but do experiment with your favorite nut. I love adding pistachios to this, and my favorite crazy combination of herbs.

Serves 2

   2 teaspoons clear honey

   2 tablespoons white wine vinegar or sherry vinegar

   1 green chile, diced

   3 good-quality tomatoes, sliced or chopped

   1 cucumber, sliced

   2 green onions, sliced

   1 garlic clove, grated

   handful of chopped purple or green basil

   handful of chopped cilantro

   handful of chopped dill

   ½ cup (2 oz/50 g) pistachio nuts or walnuts, toasted and chopped

For the dressing, mix the honey into the vinegar, add the chile, and leave for about 15 minutes to infuse.

Mix the salad vegetables, garlic, and herbs together in a bowl, then dress with the dressing, sprinkle with the pistachios, and wow!

Tomato & raspberry salad

This salad came about when Ének, a first-generation Hungarian who had settled in Georgia, picked out some extremely good tomatoes at a market in Tbilisi. Inspired by Hungarian-rooted chefs from Bar Tartine in San Francisco who do a version of this salad with sour cherries, she made one with raspberries, toasty unrefined sunflower oil, and some green coriander seeds and flower heads. I know tomatoes and raspberries sound like a combination that should just be left alone, but it actually really works if you use excellent tomatoes, although not with hard, flavorless supermarket tomatoes. The tomatoes need to be ripe, sweet, flavorsome, and juicy fruit so that they almost equal the raspberries in texture and juiciness. Strong, savory soft herbs also go very well here. Try marjoram or oregano mixed with mint or cilantro leaves, dill or tarragon – you are going for intensity here. And make sure you season it really well with good flaky sea salt.

Serves 4 as a side

- 4 large super-ripe tomatoes
- 10 firm yellow, green, and red cherry tomatoes
- 8 raspberries
- 5 black olives, pitted and torn
- 3 tablespoons unrefined sunflower oil
- sea salt flakes and freshly ground black pepper
- a few cilantro flower heads or 3 sprigs of marjoram, leaves picked
- 1 sprig of mint, leaves picked and large ones torn
- 4 sprigs of dill, chopped
- ¼ mild onion, thinly sliced

Cut the tomatoes into sections. Your tomatoes should be so ripe that you will end up with loads of juice on your chopping board. Don't throw it away, but add it to a bowl to use as part of the dressing.

Pop the cherry tomatoes onto a serving plate and scatter with the raspberries and olives.

Whisk the oil into the reserved tomato juices and pour over the salad. Season generously with some salt and pepper, and sprinkle with the herbs and onion. The juices remaining at the bottom of the salad are made for bread-mopping.

Tip If you can't find the correct sunflower oil, try another nutty oil. Mix a little sesame oil with some avocado or canola oil, or try walnut oil if you can find the good stuff.

Serdakh, or eggplants & tomatoes

I sampled this simple yet satisfying, silky vegetarian dish in Lankaran, in the southeastern region of Azerbaijan. There are many excellent eggplant and tomato dishes to be found all over the world, but this one slipped down so amazingly well and I just couldn't figure out what it was that made it extra "moreish." I've never cooked eggplants in butter before, so it was a revelation to discover that clarified butter was the key, along with a copious amount of roughly chopped and caramelized garlic. Of course, you can use oil instead, but – trust me – clarified butter makes the dish taste so unusual but strangely not heavy or buttery in a French way. Make a big pot and eat it hot or warm with a hunk of lovely bread and bunches of herbs.

Serves 2 as a main or 4 as a side

- 8–10 baby eggplants or 3 large
- 6 tablespoons (3½ oz/100 g) Clarified Butter (page 53)
- 10 garlic cloves, roughly chopped
- 6 flavorsome tomatoes, halved across the equator, or some small, colorful tomatoes, left whole, or a mixture of both
- ¾ cup (6 fl oz/200 ml) water, vegetable stock, or chicken stock
- sea salt flakes and freshly ground black pepper
- pinch of superfine sugar, if needed

TO SERVE
- lavash flatbreads or any other flatbread or regular bread, torn
- 1 small bunch of each or any of the following: dill, cilantro, basil

If you are using baby eggplants, make 2 incisions in the shape of a cross in their rounded end as if you were going to quarter them lengthwise, but don't cut into them further. I leave the stalks intact, as they look so pretty. If using large eggplants, trim and slice them about ½ inch (15 mm) thick.

Heat 2 tablespoons of the clarified butter in a heavy-bottomed flameproof casserole dish over medium heat and fry the garlic while you keep stirring it. You want it to turn deep golden and stay juicy, but not become dry or burnt. Tilt the pan so that the butter and garlic collect in one corner – this way you will confit it. It will take about 2–5 minutes. The smell will be incredible as the garlic loses its harshness and becomes soft, sweet, and gently caramelized. Take the garlic out and set aside. Do not wipe out the pan unless it looks burnt.

Heat another 2 tablespoons of the clarified butter in the same pan over medium-high heat and fry the eggplants until they are well browned all over. Be patient and the skin will blister

continued »

and the white flesh will soften, but it may take about 10 minutes – they really need to start collapsing. Take them out and set aside; you can leave them to drain on paper towels if you like. Again, do not clean the pan.

Heat another 2 tablespoons of the clarified butter in the same pan, add the tomatoes cut side down, and cook just on that side over high heat until they catch some color and the skins look wrinkled. If the tomatoes are ripe, use a pair of tongs to lift the skins off the tomatoes and discard. If they aren't, you may need to flip them, cook on the skin side briefly, and then take the skins off. Sometimes I'm too lazy to take the skins off at all.

Now return the eggplants and garlic to the pan and add the liquid. Do try using chicken stock if you are not vegetarian, as it adds an extra layer of flavor. Water is absolutely fine, though, if you want the dish to remain as hassle-free as possible. Season with salt and pepper (but go easy on the salt if you salted the eggplants previously) and add a pinch of sugar if your tomatoes are not the sweetest. Cook over medium heat until the liquid has reduced by half and the eggplants are properly cooked through, about 15 minutes.

Clarified butter

In India, the ancient holistic healing system of Ayurveda prescribes a shot of ghee, or clarified butter, as a detox agent for purifying the body, while in Azerbaijan, they love it so much that they serve their *plov* with extra for pouring over. The impoverished Molla Nasreddin – a satirical fictional character from Azerbaijani classical literature famous for mocking rich folks – and his wife were hungry one evening, so the story goes, when he asked, "To make a good *plov*, wife, what do you need?" The wife retorted, "We don't have even enough money for bread!" To which he replied, "Why don't we just dream about it . . . what would we need?" "Two pounds of rice, two pounds of ghee, and two pounds of meat," his wife said. "Darling, what are you talking about," he exclaimed, "A pound of ghee to a pound of rice – that is outrageous!" "Yes," she countered, "we are poor in reality, so just let me dream of that lovely fatty, buttery *plov*."

When you encounter *plov* recipes in this book, the quantities for clarified butter are very close to this. You can use less, but if you're like Molla's wife (like me), don't dream: go for it!

Makes about 2 lb (900 g)
6½ cups (3¼ lb/1.5 kg) unsalted butter

Preheat the oven to 200°F (100°C).

Put the butter into a pan and leave in the oven, uncovered, for the whole day. Every 2 hours, skim off the foam from the surface of the butter and discard, then pour off some of the clear liquid from the top into a container, making sure that the milk solids remain in the base of the pan.

Store the clarified butter in an airtight container in the refrigerator, where it will keep for up to about 2 weeks.

Alternatively, you can use this quick method, as we did when I worked in restaurants, but there is a greater risk of the milk solids sticking to the base of the pan: Put the butter into a large saucepan over low heat and simmer for about 30 minutes, skimming off the foam as it rises to the surface. Pour off the clear liquid into a container, leaving the milk solids behind in the pan. Store as above.

Tip *The remaining butter solids (called ayran in Azerbaijan) are amazing mixed into a bread dough such as my dough for Ossetian pies (see page 80).*

Purslane with tahini & garlic

Purslane grows in the wild all over Georgia, often spreading its delicate limbs along the soil between grapevines and even through asphalt. It is at its best in spring, but it can still be found and is often pickled in the autumn. Gia (head chef of the Pheasant's Tears restaurant in Signagi) cooked this so simply, but it was one of those dishes that I will never forget: still-crunchy purslane, a delicately balanced tahini dressing, and a little bit of raw garlic crushed over the finished dish at the very end. Tahini is not typically Georgian – a walnut dressing would be more authentically regional (you can use *pkhali* instead; see page 35) – but even Georgians are starting to creatively fuse cuisines (thank you, Yotam), and it's not hard to get tahini in Georgia. That milky, foggy morning when we tried it along with some meaty wild oyster mushrooms, its delicate flavor worked ever so well.

Serves 2 as a side

2 tablespoons lemon juice

sea salt flakes

1 teaspoon good-quality honey

1 green garlic clove or ½ ordinary garlic clove, finely grated

2 tablespoons tahini

12 oz (350 g) purslane or spinach

To make a dressing, mix the lemon juice with a good pinch of salt, then add the honey and garlic and stir to help it dissolve.

Gradually mix the lemon juice mixture into the tahini until the dressing becomes silky and pourable. Don't worry if the tahini stiffens at first – it will relax and loosen as you keep stirring and trickling in the liquid. But do add a splash of cold water if it remains stiff.

Put a saucepan of water on to boil. Drop the purslane into the water. Count to 30, drain, then cool under cold running water. Squeeze the water from the purslane, then pat it dry with paper towels.

Dress the greens with the tahini dressing and enjoy in the sun with crusty bread and some simple grilled meat or eggplants.

VARIATION

If you have the time, make some *satsivi* (see page 136) and use it in place of the tahini. Make sure that it's of pourable consistency by thinning it with some stock, lemon juice, or water.

Cauliflower, brown butter & crumbs

Aunt Nina, an Armenian growing up in Azerbaijan, was a mechanical engineering student in the 1960s. Just before the exams, sitting at her Azerbaijani friends' table with sheets of paper covered with lines and scribbles scattered around, they had a snack. No potato chips in those days, but in my view they had something a lot better – cooked cauliflower florets, a dish with melted butter and blitzed *sukhariki* or dried bread crumbs. The cauliflower was picked, dipped in the butter, then dipped in the bread crumbs and devoured. Soft, buttery, crunchy – a student snack to inspire.

Serves 2 as a revision snack

1 tablespoon olive oil

1 head of cauliflower, about 1¼ lb (550 g), divided into florets

7 tablespoons (3½ oz/100 g) unsalted butter

a few slices of stale sourdough bread

handful of finely chopped flat-leaf parsley

1 red chile, diced

1 teaspoon ground sumac (optional)

Preheat the oven to 400°F (200°C). Brush a large baking sheet with the olive oil, spread out the cauliflower florets, and roast until they are cooked through and starting to color at the edges, about 30 minutes.

Meanwhile, to make the brown butter, heat the butter in a frying pan over medium heat and let it sizzle until it starts smelling sweet and nutty. Take the pan off the heat as soon as you smell it and it turns a deep golden color, pour the contents into a cold bowl, and set aside.

To make the sourdough crumbs, blitz the bread in a blender or food processor and, if necessary, spread out on a baking sheet and place in the bottom of the oven for a few minutes to dry. Then mix with the parsley, chile, and sumac, if using.

Do your homework or exam revision/work and dip the cauliflower florets first into the brown butter, then into the sourdough crumbs. Or drizzle the butter over the cauliflower along with some cooked white beans and scatter over the crumbs to make a side dish for some grilled chicken or fish.

Tips *Alternatively, you can put the cauliflower in a roasting pan, dot loads of butter around it, and add a little chicken stock. Roast for about 30 minutes, then for the last 5 minutes of the cooking time, add the bread crumbs and sumac.*

Wild garlic, unrefined sunflower oil & vinegar

If you ever come across wild garlic or wild leeks or ramsons, try eating the bulbs and leaves as simply as this. Do be sure to seek out the best unrefined sunflower oil you can. Failing that, any other flavorsome fresh nut oil would also do nicely. Earthy wild garlic, sea salt, a little kick of acidity, raw thinly sliced onion, and a slick of nut oil – often the simplest things are the most satisfying. Serve as part of a bigger spread or as an accompaniment to some grilled pork.

Serves 2 as a side

- 10 oz (300 g) wild leek or wild garlic bulbs, well washed
- ½ small mild onion, thinly sliced
- 2 tablespoons good-quality sherry vinegar
- sea salt flakes
- 1 teaspoon granulated sugar (optional)
- 2 tablespoons unrefined sunflower oil

Blanch the bulbs in boiling water for about 1 minute, then drain and refresh under cold running water. Alternatively, steam for about 2 minutes – they should soften but still have a bit of bite.

If your onion is strong, soak the slices in some iced water for a few minutes, then drain and dry well.

Toss the bulbs in the vinegar and sprinkle with the salt to taste. Leave to pickle for 15 minutes if you have the time. I sometimes add a teaspoon of sugar at this stage, too, but it's not traditional.

Finally, scatter over the onion and drizzle over the nutty oil.

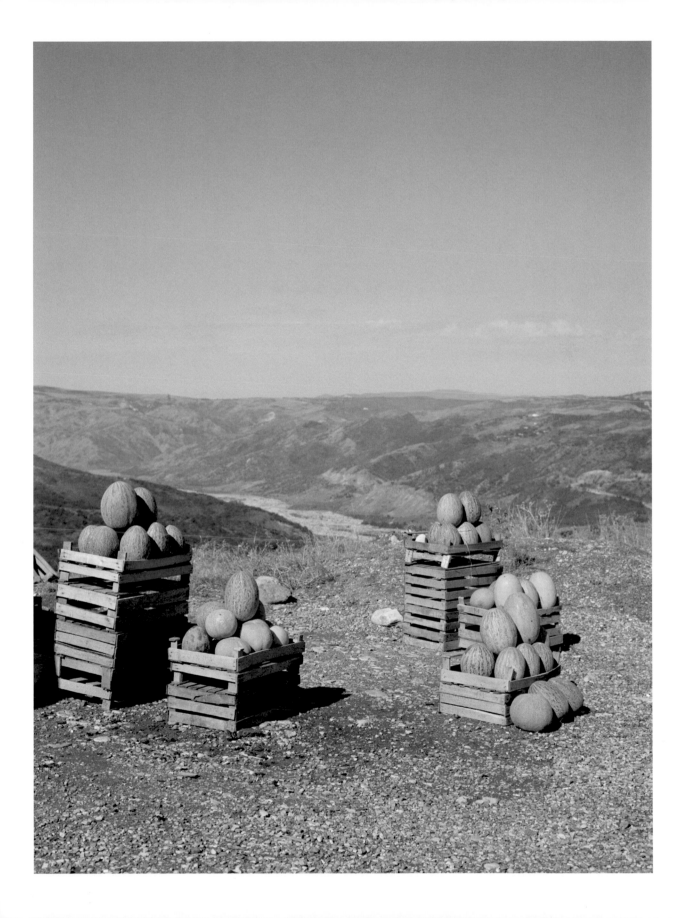

Red adjika salt

There are numerous types of *adjika*, ranging from dry garlic and chile salt to chile pastes. The commercially produced watery sauces are best avoided. My friend Ia called this recipe the *generalnaya adjika*, and it's the mother of all *adjikas*.

People rarely make this at home, and I have been told that only professionals know the secret to the perfect general *adjika*. But I am never deterred in such situations, so I grabbed a 6½-pound tub at the market in Zugdidi and brought it back to London to begin my experiment. You will need to source some good blue fenugreek, or what the Georgians call *utskhosuneli*, which is used in numerous dishes in this book. It is extremely versatile, so just apply your imagination and creative flair with abandon. If all fails, you will find details for an online supplier of the ready-made salt on page 234. Use it sprinkled over eggs or in a salad dressing (see page 16).

Makes about 1⅔ lb (750 g)
- 7 oz (200 g) ground blue fenugreek
- 3½ oz (100 g) ground coriander
- 2¼ oz (65 g) dried marigold petals or powder

- 40 garlic cloves, peeled
- 3½ oz (100 g) cayenne pepper (or the same quantity of fresh red chiles if you want to make a wet paste – see variation below)
- ⅔ cup (7 oz/200 g) sea salt flakes

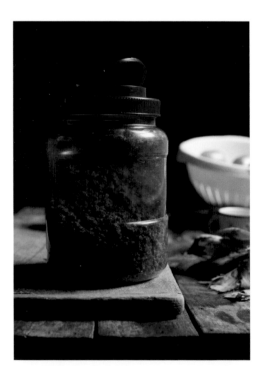

Bash everything together using a mortar and pestle, or pass through a meat mincer, which is what's mostly used these days, as it results in neat red salt pellets that keep very well out of the refrigerator.

What you will end up with essentially is a flavored salt, so use it sparingly. It will keep for a couple of months in an airtight container in a cool, dry place.

VARIATION
To make a wet paste version, Wet Red Adjika, simply use fresh red chiles instead of the cayenne. Store the paste in the refrigerator in a sterilized airtight jar, adding a thin film of oil on top if you want it to keep for longer.

Svaneti salt

Georgians love their slightly moist garlic- and chile-flavored salts, and *Svaneti* salt is justifiably famous in the country, as it is such a delight – garlicky, herby, and a little spicy. This is particularly good stirred into Homemade *Matsoni* (page 29) or plain yogurt, or used as a seasoning for anything you like. Try it sprinkled on Fresh Homemade Cheese (page 107) and ripe tomatoes or cucumbers.

Makes 1¼ lb (550 g)
- 1 cup (10½ oz/300 g) sea salt flakes
- 1 tablespoon coriander seeds, ground into a powder
- 1 tablespoon ground blue fenugreek
- 1 teaspoon caraway seeds
- 1 teaspoon powdered dried marigold petals
- 1 tablespoon red pepper flakes or hot paprika
- 13 garlic cloves, crushed

Mix the salt with all the dry spices, then add to a blender or food processor and blitz with the crushed garlic.

Transfer the salt to a large airtight container and store in a cool, dark place. This quantity should last you a couple of years, but is best consumed within 6 months.

Tip *If sourcing these specific spices is too much of a chore, there are suppliers that sell ready-made Svaneti salt – see page 234 for details.*

Samegrelo roast pumpkin & red adjika

Sweet caramelized pumpkin or squash smothered in *adjika*, a spicy, salty chile paste with blue fenugreek, was a revelation to me. Use the best-quality nuts you can find – walnuts are wonderful when in season.

Serves 4 as a side

  1 small pumpkin or butternut squash, unpeeled

  2 tablespoons canola or olive oil

  sea salt flakes

  2 tablespoons Wet Red Adjika (page 62) or store-bought

  handful of nuts, such as walnuts, pecans, or hazelnuts, ground

TO SERVE

  3 tablespoons (1¾ oz/50 g) Homemade Matsoni (page 29) or plain yogurt, thinned with 1 tablespoon water

  handful of soft herbs, such as cilantro, dill, basil, chervil, and fennel tops

Preheat the oven to 400°F (200°C).

Cut the pumpkin or squash in half lengthwise and then cut into half-moons ¾ inch (2 cm) thick. Spread out over a baking sheet, drizzle over the oil and season lightly with salt. Roast until the pumpkin or squash starts caramelizing at the edges, 30–40 minutes.

Mix the *adjika* paste with the ground nuts, then spread it all over the pumpkin or squash. Reduce the oven to 325°F (160°C), and roast for a further 10 minutes.

Serve drizzled with the *matsoni* and your favorite herbs alongside some grilled meat and a fresh salad.

Tips *If you can't be bothered to make adjika but haven't been able to source a decent version of the store-bought stuff (not the watery tomato-based adjikas you can find in Russian shops), use a good-quality harissa. You can also make a warm salad with the pumpkin or squash – just add some bitter leaves or watercress.*

Savory peach & tarragon salad

We are used to tarragon in creamy sauces in the West, but mainly just with chicken, and it remains such an underused herb, often declared too strong and dominant. But Georgians love it and it finds its way into many, many dishes. We made this in Tbilisi in June, inspired by the gorgeous local produce. A savory salad made only with fruit may seem unusual, but it works. Sour gooseberries or grapes combined with sweet peaches (or nectarines), along with savory tarragon and salt, makes a dream accompaniment to some grilled pork or lamb chops, or roasted meaty summer squashes.

Serves 2 as a side

  2 peaches, pitted and sliced
  ½ cup (1¾ oz/50 g) gooseberries or grapes (or 4 tart plums, pitted and sliced)
  ½ small bunch of tarragon, leaves picked (or a few fennel fronds)
  2 tablespoons lemon juice
  ¼ small red chile, seeded and diced
  ½ teaspoon superfine sugar or honey
  1 small garlic clove, grated
  sea salt flakes and freshly ground black pepper

Arrange the peaches and gooseberries on a plate. Mix the tarragon leaves with the lemon juice, fresh chile, sugar, garlic, some salt, and a generous pinch of pepper, then pour the dressing over the fruit and serve.

VARIATION

Mix a handful of pumpkin seeds with ½ tablespoon of maple syrup, a pinch of red pepper flakes, and some salt, spread them out onto a parchment-lined baking sheet, and roast in a preheated 350°F (180°C) oven for 5 minutes. Remove from the oven, leave to cool, then use as a savory topping.

Turshulash-style roots & beans

I love when traditional recipes inspire or are given a slight makeover. Zulya was a piano teacher at a conservatory in Baku (which she still does part-time), but 16 years ago she became so obsessed with baking that she opened a small bakery in her garage. She decorated it with fabrics to make it look exotically (for Baku) European. They now have five beautiful pastry shops across Baku and are some of the loveliest people I've ever met. Zulya's mum comes from Lankaran, in southeastern Azerbaijan close to the Iranian border, and she often draws inspiration for her dishes from her mother's heritage. *Turshulash*, which literally translates as "sour dinner," is one such dish, a gorgeous seven-bean (or rather legume, including chickpeas and green and red lentils), corn, carrot, and beet combo from Lankaran. She calls this salad "*turshulash* Z-style," which annoys her husband Rufat (almost endearingly, as he is such a lovely guy), as he says it's a false representation and demands that she find a new name for it. But I'm with Zulya – traditional-inspired dishes should hint at their origins.

Serves 6 as a side

1 lb (500 g) celery root, peeled and cut into ¾-inch (2-cm) dice

1 lb (500 g) Chioggia or regular beets, peeled and cut into ½-inch (1-cm) dice

sea salt flakes

2 ripe tomatoes, grated

2¼ lb (1 kg) squash, peeled and cut into ¾-inch (2-cm) dice

9 oz (250 g) quinces, peeled, cored, and diced

2 tablespoons maple syrup or honey

3 tablespoons Alycha paste (*tursha*) or tamarind paste

14-oz (400-g) can red kidney beans, drained

Put the celery root and beets into a saucepan, cover with cold water, then add some salt and the tomato pulp and bring to a boil. Reduce the heat and simmer until the roots are tender, about 15 minutes.

Using a slotted spoon, remove the vegetables from the water in the saucepan and set aside. Add the squash and quinces to the pan. Bring to a boil, then reduce the heat and simmer until the squash is tender and quince is soft but still a little al dente, about 15 minutes.

Remove the squash and quince to the bowl with the other vegetables. Add the maple syrup and Alycha paste to the vegetable-cooking liquid and reduce over high heat until only about ¾ cup (6 fl oz/200 ml) is left in the pan. Remove from the heat, return the vegetables to the pan and stir them through, then leave to cool completely. You should end up with a kind of a salad with a loose dressing that tastes strongly of all the vegetables and has a sweet and sour note. Mix the beans through and serve as a side dish or mixed with some bitter leaves like a winter salad.

Herb kükü

"I tried an Azerbaijani herby omelette called kükü!" I announced excitedly. "That dish was originally Iranian!" was Sabrina Ghayour's response – there is no escaping her intensely Persian focus. While I agree with her that this dish definitely has Persian roots, it is also treasured in neighboring Azerbaijan. I really love the name (it sounds so playful), love how herby it is (it's mostly herbs held together by a little egg), and love the sprinkling of sumac on top. You can fry it in oil if you wish, but I do love soft herbs cooked in butter – there is so much satisfaction to be had from a combination of fresh, fragrant flavor, creamy dairy, and eggs. Play around with the combination of soft herbs; there are endless variants to enjoy – I often use watercress, spring onion, sorrel, spinach, or wild garlic. Serve with flatbreads, a simple tomato salad (see page 47), and some plain yogurt with chopped cucumber, chile, salt, and a tiny bit of garlic.

Serves 4

5 oz (150 g) mixed soft herbs, such as cilantro, dill, purple or green basil, tarragon, and chives

4 eggs

sea salt flakes

1 garlic clove, finely grated

3 spring onions or green onions, minced

1½ tablespoons (¾ oz/20 g) Clarified Butter (page 53) or ordinary butter and a drop of vegetable oil

½ teaspoon ground sumac

Remove any tough stalks from your mixture of herbs, then finely chop the softer stalks together with the leaves.

Whisk the eggs with some salt and the garlic, then stir in all the chopped herbs and green onions.

Heat the clarified butter in a 9-inch (23-cm) diameter frying pan over medium-low heat and add the herby eggs. Cook, without touching it, until the eggs are just set and the underside develops a golden crust, about 5 minutes.

Now comes the tricky bit. To flip the kükü, cover the pan with a big plate, turn it upside-down onto the plate, then slide the kükü back into the pan. Continue cooking until the other side is golden, 1 minute, then remove from the heat and slide it onto a serving plate. Sprinkle the sumac on the top, and serve.

VARIATION

You can also add a handful of lightly toasted and crushed walnuts to the kükü. For a winter version of the dish, use thinly sliced Swiss chard or beet greens or sweet green cabbage instead of the herbs.

I witnessed one of the most impressive examples of bread-making I have ever seen in my life in the tiny village of Andriatsminda. Galina, who is a prolific farmer and a perfect example of the Georgian *dedakatsi* (an impossibly strong, if self-sacrificial, Georgian woman), had her own baking room – essentially a dark basement space with a wood-fired oven. Without wasting any of the heat that the oven provided, she baked four different types of bread, each taking its turn when the temperature of the oven was just right for it. First, when the oven was at its hottest, a type of flatbread went in, called *lavashi*. When that was cooked and the fire had become a little less fierce, the second bread went in, one with a hole in the center called *shoti*. After that, her incredible *khachapouri* were ready, and finally, when the oven began to cool down, she put in the largest bread, *somini*, which needs low and slow baking. The breads were then cooled on a rack made out of hazelnut branches. This ingenious way of economizing on energy, utilizing every bit of power that the burning wood can provide, is incredible.

flour & ash

Marina's kada lobiani

There are many ways to make *khachapouri*, but I loved the technique I saw in Akhaltsikhe in southern Georgia the most, where it was folded a few times with either butter or pork lard added between the folds, to create the most gorgeous, flaky flatbreads. Here the breads are stuffed with a dried fava bean and caramelized onion paste.

Makes 3

DOUGH

1 egg

6 tablespoons (3½ oz/100 g) Homemade Matsoni (page 29) or plain yogurt

½ cup plus 2 tablespoons (5 fl oz/150 ml) lukewarm milk

2¼ teaspoons (¼ oz/7 g) instant yeast

1 teaspoon fine sea salt

½ tablespoon honey

5 cups (1⅓ lb/600 g) all-purpose flour , plus extra for kneading and dusting

1 tablespoon sunflower oil, for oiling

FILLING

1 cup (7 oz/200 g) dried fava or red kidney beans, soaked overnight in cold water

2 fresh or dried bay leaves

2 carrots, roughly chopped

2 celery ribs, roughly chopped

5 onions, 1 halved, 4 thinly sliced

4 oz (100 g) piece of pancetta rind or smoked bacon (optional)

⅔ cup (5 oz/150 g) unsalted butter, softened

2 large garlic cloves, finely chopped

sea salt flakes and freshly ground black pepper

GLAZE

1 egg

6 tablespoons (3½ oz/100 g) plain yogurt

To make the dough, mix the egg, *matsoni*, and milk in a large bowl, then add the yeast, salt, and honey. Gradually add the flour, mixing it in first with a spoon and then your hand. You need enough flour so that the dough comes together but is still a little wet. Oil the dough, cover the bowl in plastic wrap or a damp kitchen towel, then leave the dough to rise in the bowl for about an hour. It will double in size and will be very airy, soft, and voluptuous.

Meanwhile, make the filling. Drain the soaked beans and add to a saucepan with 2 qt (2 L) water along with the bay leaves, carrots, celery, and halved onion. Bring to a boil, skim off the foam that rises to the surface, and cook until the beans are really soft, 1 hour. Add the pancetta rind to the beans for the last 30–40 minutes of the cooking time if you want your beans to have a lovely smoky flavor. If you have bacon rather than pancetta, use it in the next step.

continued »

In a frying pan over medium heat, heat ¼ cup (2 oz/50 g) of the butter – or the bacon, if using, until the fat starts to render – add the thinly sliced onions and cook gently, stirring from time to time, until they are deep golden, about 10 minutes. When they are close to that stage, add the garlic and cook for a few more minutes.

Strain the beans and discard all the vegetables and pancetta rind (if used). Blitz the beans, the onion mixture (leave in the bacon if used), and a little salt and pepper in a blender or food processor. Taste the mixture – it should be sweet and well seasoned. If you wanted to add some of your favorite spices here, such as coriander seeds, toast and then grind them and go ahead, but I like it just as it is.

Divide the dough into 3 pieces. Take one piece of dough and roll it out on a lightly floured work surface into a 12-inch (30-cm) round. Take a tablespoonful of soft butter and, using your hand, spread it all over the round. Then fold the right side of the round in and then the left side over it to create a narrow rectangle. If you dare, butter the rectangle again and roll it up. Leave to proof, seam-side down and covered with a damp kitchen towel, while you tackle the other two dough rounds.

To fill the bread, dust the dough and your work surface with flour and roll the dough pieces out into a 8 x 12–inch (20 x 30–cm) rectangle. Spread about 1 cup (8 oz/225 g) of the bean paste in a thin layer all over each bread. Now roll each piece of dough up into a long sausage and twist into coils to create snail-like shapes. Gently, roll your pin over the snails, to seal the layers together. If your dough is soft, each coil will merge together into a flatbread with a spiral pattern inside. Put them onto separate baking sheets lined with parchment paper and leave to proof and expand somewhere cool for an hour, or freeze them to be baked later.

Meanwhile, preheat the oven to 400°F (200°C).

Lightly beat the egg for the glaze, mix in the yogurt, and brush over the breads to glaze, then bake for 10–15 minutes. Serve the breads freshly baked with a simple salad for a lunch or quick dinner after work.

Tip *Once you are at the stage when the dough has been filled and you have left it to proof, you can freeze it and then glaze and bake from frozen at the highest temperature in your oven.*

Opposite: *Galina's* shoti *(above) and pork lard* khachapouri *breads.*

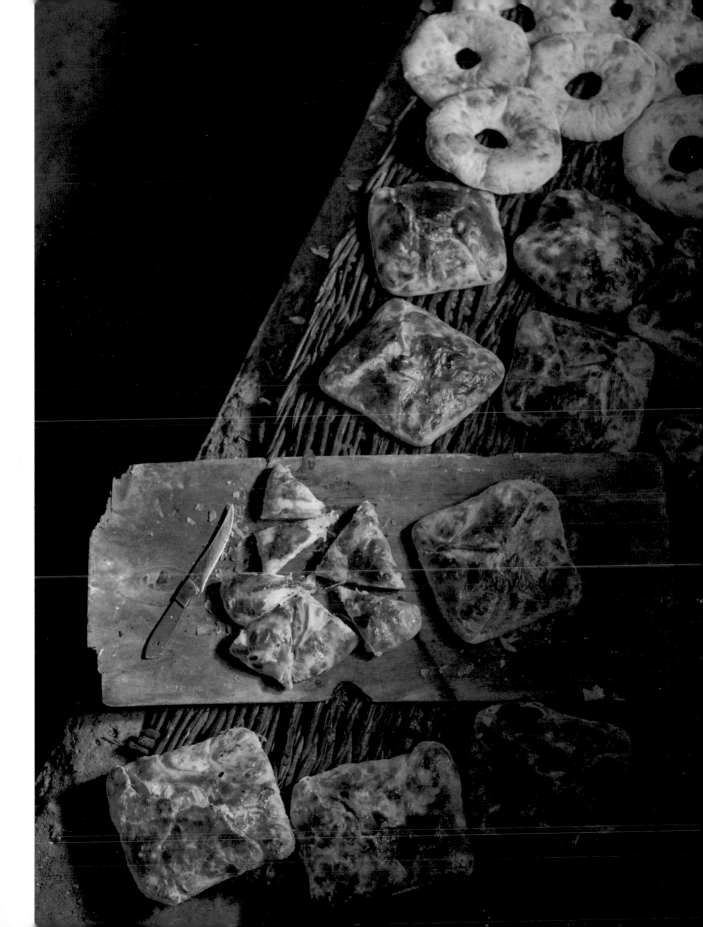

Ossetian beet top and cheese pies

I grew up with Ossetian pies. Our friend Svetlana is married to an Ossetian, and she was taught how to make them by her husband's mother in the mountains, then brought them to Ukraine and wowed us. A pile of them, some with meat, some with cheese, was exotic and familiar at the same time. In Ossetia they are traditionally served three at a time, sometimes round, sometimes triangular, each with a different filling and meant to represent fire, water, and earth – most definitely an ancient tradition, originating in paganism. Pagan pies, connecting us with the elements and the universe – I'm in.

Makes 3 large pies (each pie serves 2–3)

OSSETIAN PIE DOUGH

- 2¼ teaspoons (¼ oz/7 g) instant yeast
- 1 teaspoon clear honey
- ½ cup plus 2 tablespoons (5 fl oz/150 ml) lukewarm kefir
- ½ cup plus 2 tablespoons (5 fl oz/150 ml) lukewarm milk
- 4½ cups (1¼ lb/550 g) organic white bread flour, plus extra for dusting
- 1½ teaspoons fine sea salt
- ¼ cup (2 oz/50 g) unsalted butter, to glaze

BEET TOPS & CHEESE FILLING

- 1½ tablespoons (¾ oz/20 g) unsalted butter
- 12 oz (350 g) beet greens, stalks, and leaves (or use Swiss chard)
- 2 garlic cloves, finely chopped
- grated zest of ½ lemon (optional)
- 7 oz (200 g) raclette or Ogleshield cheese, coarsely grated
- 5 oz (150 g) feta cheese, crumbled
- sea salt flakes and freshly ground black pepper
- 4 oz (100 g) green onions, chopped
- 1 tablespoon chopped dill

For the dough, mix the yeast and honey into the lukewarm kefir and milk in a jug and leave until you see bubbles appearing on the surface, 10 minutes or so.

Pour the yeast mixture into a large bowl, then gradually add half the flour and mix together until you have a soft, very wet dough. The reason why we are looking for a very wet dough here is because it will make it easier to add the salt to the dough later; if you add the salt too early, the yeast will struggle to multiply.

Cover the bowl with plastic wrap or a damp kitchen towel and leave to rise in a warm place for about 40 minutes.

Now make the brown butter to glaze the pies later. Have a heatproof bowl at the ready. Heat the 1½ tablespoons butter in a saucepan over medium-low heat until it starts foaming and then changes color to deep golden and starts smelling nutty. Immediately tip it from the hot pan into the bowl; otherwise, it can continue cooking and may burn. Set aside for later.

To make the filling, thinly slice the stalks of the beet greens and roughly chop the leaves. Heat the ¼ cup butter in a pan over low heat, add the garlic, and cook for a few minutes. Then add the beet stalks and leaves and cook for a further 5 minutes or so – you are looking for the stalks to soften, but still retain texture. Add the lemon zest at the very end, if using, then give it all a good stir and leave to cool.

Preheat the oven to 425°F (220°C). Line 2 baking sheets with baking parchment.

Once the beet mixture is cool, mix it with the cheeses, season well with salt and pepper and add the green onions and dill. Mix thoroughly and shape into 3 balls.

Flour your hands, then knead the fine sea salt and some of the remaining flour into the risen dough until it stops sticking to your hands. It should still be very soft and pillowy, though. Divide the dough into 3 even pieces. Flatten each piece with your hand and roll out on a lightly floured work surface into rounds about ¾ inch (2 cm) thick. Place a cheese ball in the center of each dough round. Bring the edges of the dough up over the filling, pleating as you go, and pinch the ends together really well at the top to secure like a money bag. Sprinkle a little flour over the top and flip the pouch over, then flatten the pouch gently with your hand, spreading the filling inside all the way to the edges. You can also use your rolling pin gently to flatten it a little further.

Pop the pies onto the lined baking sheets. Make a slit in the middle of each pie to let the steam out, and bake for 15 minutes. The dough should be golden and the pies' bottoms should be dry. Brush the pies with the brown butter as soon as they are out of the oven, and eat immediately.

Try different fillings for your Ossetian pies, using them in the same way as the beet tops and cheese filling (see next two pages).

continued »

All fillings will fill 3 pies. To scale up or down, you simply need the same weight filling as Ossetian pie dough.

Davondjin . . . with wild garlic & cheese filling

1½ tablespoons unsalted butter

1 lb (500 g) wild garlic, chopped, or 1 lb (500 g) spinach, chopped plus 8 crushed garlic cloves

7 oz (200 g) Fresh Homemade Cheese (page 107) or ricotta cheese (strained if too wet)

7 oz (200 g) feta cheese, crumbled

sea salt flakes and freshly ground black pepper

Heat the butter in a large frying pan, add the wild garlic (or the spinach and garlic cloves), and sauté over low heat for a few minutes, then leave to cool.

Mix the cooled wild garlic with the cheeses and season well. Divide the mixture into 3 portions and use to fill the Ossetian pie dough (see page 80).

Kabuskadjin . . . with shredded cabbage filling

1½ tablespoons (¾ oz/20 g) unsalted butter

3 onions, thinly sliced

5 garlic cloves, sliced

3 tablespoons tomato paste

1⅓ lb (600 g) sweetheart (pointed) or napa or green cabbage, shredded

sea salt flakes and freshly ground black pepper

Heat the butter in a large frying pan, add the onions, and cook gently until soft and starting to become golden, 10–15 minutes.

Add the garlic, stir in the tomato paste, and cook over medium heat for a few minutes, then add the cabbage and cook until the cabbage softens, 5–8 minutes. Leave the mixture to cool, then season well. Divide the mixture into 3 portions and use to fill the Ossetian pie dough (see page 80).

Baldjin . . . with sour cherry filling

1⅓ lb (600 g) sour cherries, pitted (or use sweet cherries with a squeeze of lemon juice)

1½ cups (10½ oz/300 g) granulated sugar

Mix the cherries with the sugar. Divide the mixture into 3 portions and use to fill the Ossetian pie dough (see page 80).

Kartifdjin . . . with potato & cheese filling

2½ cups (1⅓ lb/600 g) cold leftover mashed potato (with milk and butter)
10½ oz (300 g) melty cheese, such as raclette or Ogleshield, grated
3 eggs
sea salt flakes, if needed, and freshly ground black pepper

Mix the mashed potato, grated cheese, and eggs together really well, then taste and add a little salt if needed and some pepper – you want the mixture to be well seasoned.

Divide the mixture into 3 portions and use to fill the Ossetian pie dough (see page 80).

Nastdzhyn . . . with squash & onion filling

1¾ lb (800 g) butternut squash or pumpkin, peeled, seeded,
and coarsely grated (1⅓ lb/600 g grated weight)
sea salt flakes
4 tablespoons mild olive oil
3 onions, finely diced
5 tablespoons pomegranate molasses
sea salt flakes and freshly ground black pepper
1 tablespoon chopped mint (or other fresh herb of your choice)

Mix the grated squash with a pinch of salt really well with your hands and set aside.

Heat the oil in a large frying pan, add the onions, and sweat until they start to soften and caramelize.

Add the grated squash or pumpkin to the pan along with the pomegranate molasses, then season to taste. Cook over medium heat, stirring from time to time, until the squash softens, about 5 minutes.

Leave the mixture to cool, then add the mint. Divide the mixture into 3 portions and use to fill the Ossetian pie dough (see page 80).

Khinkali

Khinkali is a national Georgian dish. It is said to have originated in the Kazbegi and Tusheti mountains in the northeast, but it is now found all over the country. The dumplings are normally made with a mixture of beef and pork or lamb, but when we visited the hills of Akhaltsikhe, Khatuna and her mother Raya told us that they used to make them using goose meat. Whatever meat you use, the trick is to mince the meat for the filling by hand and to have a rather liquid mixture – the wetter the filling, the more juice each dumpling will contain. Ketino Sujashvili, who lives in the Kazbegi mountains and who taught me this recipe (pictured opposite), screwed the little end off the dough as soon as she shaped the dumpling, but in restaurants, they traditionally leave the tip of the khinkali in place so that their guests can niftily hold it in their fingers and discard it while the main bit is eaten. I like the little tip, though, so I don't throw it away. The dumplings should and will be full of juice inside, so be careful not to burn your mouth on the juice or to spill it.

Traditionally, khinkali are eaten just with some black pepper ground on top, but I don't bat an eyelid before drizzling them with a little melted butter or even brown butter (see page 80). If you don't finish all of them at one sitting, don't despair. They are not at their best when cold, but are perfect refried in a little butter until crispy. Then you could serve them with Tina's Fresh Tkemali (page 23) or some Satsebeli (page 19).

Makes 25–30 khinkali

DOUGH

1 tablespoon sunflower oil

2½–3 cups (10½–12 oz/300–350 g) all-purpose flour, plus extra for dusting

FILLING

8 oz (250 g) equal parts beef and pork (nice fatty cuts)

1¼ cups (5 oz/150 g) onion, finely diced

2 small garlic cloves, crushed

¼ teaspoon cayenne pepper

1 green chile, diced (if you like less heat, leave this out)

1 teaspoon good-quality black peppercorns, freshly ground

sea salt flakes

To make the dough, pour ⅔ cup (5 fl oz/150 ml) water and the oil into a bowl, then gradually mix in the flour.

Knead the dough on a well-floured work surface for a good 5 minutes to get the gluten to develop. The dough will be very tight and this is what you want, as it will need to hold quite a substantial filling and you don't want it ripping in the pan. Wrap the dough in plastic wrap and leave to rest in the refrigerator for at least 15–30 minutes – leave it for longer if possible.

continued »

To make the filling, using a very sharp knife, cut the meat into very thin strips and then cut the strips across. You should end up with very small pieces of meat. You can use a meat cleaver to hand-mince the meat if you are confident with it.

Mix the meat with the onion, garlic, 3 tablespoons cold water, the cayenne, green chile (if using), black pepper, and some salt. The pepper is used here as a spice, and you should be able to taste its heat in the resulting *khinkali*. Leave the mixture to stand for about 15 minutes, then add 3 more tablespoons cold water and leave to stand again for about 10 minutes. If it's your first time, add less water – it will be much easier to practice shaping the dumplings.

Roll out the rested dough on a floured work surface into a 14-inch (35-cm) square sheet about ⅛ inch (2.5 mm) thick. Bear in mind that you will be rolling the dough out more once the rounds are cut out, and also that you will be using a rather wet and heavy filling, so the dough mustn't be too thin – otherwise, the dumplings will burst in the pan. *Khinkali* are sturdy dumplings – there is none of the delicacy of the ethereal *raviolo* here.

Using a glass about 3 inches (7.5 cm) in diameter, stamp out rounds from the dough. Roll each round out a little thinner, about 3½ inches (9 cm) in diameter.

If making for the first time, start with less filling than you should ideally put in, as it will be easier to practice shaping the dumplings. If you have made them before, place a tablespoonful of the filling in the center of each round. Using the tips of your fingers, start bringing the edges of the round up over the filling, pleating and pinching firmly as you go, resulting in a money bag shape. Pinch the "neck" of the money bag really well, and either remove the tip or leave it in place. They say that 19 pleats make a truly perfect *khinkali*. I can manage about 12 without straining too much, and that works fine for me. Keep any filled *khinkali* covered with a damp kitchen towel to prevent them from drying out before cooking.

Bring a large saucepan of salted water to a rolling boil and cook the *khinkali*, in batches of 8, for about 8 minutes – they will float to the top when ready. Remove with a slotted spoon, drain well, and serve hot.

VARIATIONS

Khinkali are supposed to be spicy, but if you don't enjoy spice, adjust the flavor to your taste. You can soak the seeded green chiles in iced water to get rid of some of the heat while retaining the chile flavor. Ketino added all sorts of beautiful flavorings, such as wild caraway and thyme; or garlic and chopped cilantro, although others say that such additions aren't right. But cooking isn't about rules. As long as your *khinkali* are well seasoned and full of juice, they're a winner.

Qutab three ways

Baku has changed. The old Soviet quarters are almost completely destroyed, and we are told that people are forced out of their houses and buildings to make space for companies keen to erect another Dubai-style skyscraper. My brother and I are hopeful that our Aunt's old building is still there. We want to see it – the unusually large balconies, the courtyard, the kids playing chess. Maybe; unlikely. We set off all the same, both determined and hopelessly romantic. A message comes from Aunt Nina saying, "Flat no 1, house 10, Yusuf Zade Street." We check at the hotel and they tell us that all the streets were renamed in the 1990s. This street no longer exists. Rubbish. We run outside and head for the taxi driver with the most silver hair. He only vaguely remembers. "Let's give it a go." We drive into an area that seems to be on the cusp of the sprawling shiny skyscrapers, about to be swallowed up by the modern grandeur within the next few years no doubt. We do not lose hope. Our driver runs out and asks an even more seasoned driver about Yusuf Zade Street. He points at a street that seems to have no ending. We thank them both and set off. Crumbling buildings, washing flapping in the wind, abandoned chairs, more crumbling walls. People keep pointing north; we are at the wrong end of the street. We continue walking and walking. Some of the old Soviet buildings have tiny newly built extensions that serve as little street-food stalls. Women keep flipping flatbreads. We must have been walking for over an hour and, now starving, my brother finally makes a decision. Here, we eat here. "What are you making?" I ask. "Kutaby!" *Qutabs* – delicious thin flatbreads stuffed with different fillings – herbs, meat, pumpkin, and pomegranates – the options are endless. The woman in a flowery summer dress and headband passes us three of them, fresh and hot, through a barred window, one with soft herbs, one with offal, and one with pumpkin. It was one of the best meals we've had in Azerbaijan, hands down. No doubt accentuated by the sense of adventure, nostalgia, a long walk, and hunger, but still, it was a snack I will never forget.

Makes 10 medium qutabs
  1 egg, lightly beaten
  pinch of fine sea salt
  4 cups (1 lb/500 g) all-purpose flour, plus extra for kneading and dusting

filling of choice (see pages 89–90)
1½ tablespoons unsalted butter, melted (optional)

To make the dough, mix ¾ cup (6 fl oz/200 ml) cold water, the egg, and the salt together in a bowl, then gradually add the flour, combining it with your hands. Tip the dough out onto a well-floured work surface and start kneading it. The dough should be firm but not too dry and should stop sticking to your hands after kneading in some extra flour.

continued »

An extra-large qutab Lizgin-style on the side of the road in Qebele.

Divide the dough into 10 ball-shaped pieces and leave to rest in the refrigerator for 30 minutes, covered with a damp kitchen towel or plastic wrap.

Roll out each piece of dough on a lightly floured work surface as thinly as you can into a 8-inch (20-cm) round.

Spread 2 oz (50 g) of the filling on the bottom half of each round, then fold the top half over the filling and pinch the edges together to create a half-moon shape.

Heat a large frying pan over medium-high heat until hot – don't use any fat, as we are dry-frying here. Add 1–2 *qutabs* and cook until the flatbread is golden and speckled with dark blisters, 2–3 minutes on each side. If you are using a raw meat filling, try to cook the *qutabs* at a slightly lower temperature, making sure that the filling is thoroughly cooked through.

Brush with the melted butter after cooking, if you like.

Tip *Some garlicky plain yogurt with mint, a squeeze of lemon juice, and a dribble of hot chile sauce is also delicious served with the qutabs.*

Lamb, onion & molasses filling

Some soaked fruit leather (see page 216) is normally used in this filling to add a little acidity, but if you can't make or buy it, simply add some pomegranate molasses instead. Meat provenance is very important here, as the filling is just cooked. This is also lovely when a combination of lamb and beef or beef and pork is used, but of course porkiness is my addition; in primarily Muslim Azerbaijan, it's all about the lamb.

12 oz (350 g) ground lamb (or 50/50 beef and pork mix)

1 cup (5 oz/150 g) finely diced or grated onion

1 tablespoon ground cumin

1 tablespoon ground coriander

1 tablespoon dried mint

1 tablespoon pomegranate molasses

1½ teaspoons fine sea salt

TO SERVE
melted unsalted butter, for brushing

ground sumac, for sprinkling

Mix all the ingredients except the butter and sumac together.

Test the filling for seasoning by frying a little piece of the mixture in a small pan until cooked through and then tasting – it should be well seasoned.

Use the mixture to fill each dough round and then cook them following the method on page 88.

Brush the cooked *qutabs* with a little melted butter as soon as they come out of the pan and sprinkle with some sumac.

VARIATION
You can also use Kuchmachi (page 138) to fill the *qutab* dough if you have leftovers – simply chop it really finely before using.

Herb & cheese filling

You can lose the cheese and just up the amount of herbs here, whisking a little egg yolk into the herb filling, but this will make a much thinner layer of filling. You can also vary the combination of herbs, or use sorrel instead of some of the herbs, or spinach or even watercress!

continued »

14 oz (400 g) feta cheese, crumbled

3½ oz (100 g) green onions, finely chopped

1½ tablespoons chopped dill

1½ tablespoons chopped purple (or green) basil

1½ tablespoons chopped tarragon

1½ tablespoons chopped cilantro

sea salt flakes, to taste, if needed

TO SERVE

melted unsalted butter, for brushing

ground sumac, for sprinkling

Using your hands, mix all the ingredients except the butter and sumac together thoroughly, adding a little salt if the cheese isn't salty enough.

Use the mixture to fill each dough round and then cook them following the method on page 88.

Brush the cooked *qutabs* with a little melted butter as soon as they come out of the pan, and sprinkle over some sumac.

Squash & pomegranate filling

14 oz (400 g) butternut squash or pumpkin, peeled, seeded, and coarsely grated

2 teaspoons sea salt flakes, plus extra if needed

2 tablespoons mild olive oil

⅔ cup (3½ oz/100 g) finely diced onion

large handful of pomegranate seeds

1 tablespoon chopped dill

1 tablespoon chopped cilantro

TO SERVE

6 tablespoons (3½ oz/100 g) plain yogurt

½ garlic clove, crushed

pinch of ground sumac

Mix the grated squash with the salt really well with your hands, then set aside.

Heat the oil in a large frying pan over medium heat, add the onion, and sweat until starting to soften and caramelize, 10–15 minutes.

Squeeze the liquid out of the grated squash, add it to the frying pan, and cook over medium-low heat, stirring from time to time, until softened, about 5 minutes.

Transfer the mixture to a bowl and leave to cool, then add the pomegranate seeds, herbs, and a little more salt if needed. Mix everything together gently so as not to burst the pomegranate seeds.

Use the mixture to fill each dough round and then cook them following the method on page 88. Serve with the yogurt flavored with the crushed garlic, sprinkled with the sumac.

Aniko's tarragon pie

There are as many versions of this pie as there are women in Georgia, and this recipe from Aniko, the mother of my friend Nino, was a revelation to me. Aniko had kept it a secret her whole life – she wouldn't have revealed it under torture! Nino misses her mum who is now sadly gone, and was unsure about revealing her secret recipe to the thousands of people who may read this book. However, when we met at her childhood home to cook this pie, at midday we were starving and had some cheese, salad, and bread along with a drop of wine. When I poured the second shot of wine (we couldn't find bigger glasses), I clumsily overfilled Nino's glass, spilling it all over the tablecloth and the snow-white cheese. Embarrassed, I apologized, but Nino's face lit up, as in Georgia, this is a sign that the ancestors who used to live in the house are happy to receive their descendants and guests. It was a gorgeous omen, making us feel like, finally, mystically, we were allowed to share the recipe.

Serves 6–8

PASTRY

6 tablespoons (3 oz/100 g) cold unsalted butter, diced, plus extra for greasing

3 cups (12 oz/350 g) all-purpose flour, plus extra for dusting

6 tablespoons (3½ oz/100 g) Homemade Matsoni (page 29) or kefir or plain yogurt

2 eggs, lightly beaten

½ teaspoon fine sea salt

4 big bunches of tarragon (about 5 oz/ 150 g), leaves picked and finely chopped

6 green onions, finely chopped

3 hard-boiled eggs, shelled and chopped

1 teaspoon sea salt flakes, or to taste

2 egg yolks, beaten, for glazing

For the pastry, rub the cold butter into the flour in a bowl until it resembles bread crumbs. Then add the *matsoni*, lightly beaten eggs, and salt and mix together well. Knead the dough, adding more flour if the pastry is still too wet – you are looking for a soft but not particularly damp dough. Wrap in plastic wrap and leave to rest and firm in the refrigerator for 15 minutes.

Meanwhile, mix all the ingredients for the filling together.

Preheat the oven to 350°F (180°C). Grease a 9½-inch (24-cm) round shallow cake pan or pie dish.

Divide the pastry dough in half. Roll out one half on a lightly floured work surface and use it to line the greased pan or dish. Add the filling and spread it evenly over the base of the pastry. Roll out the other piece of dough, lay it over the top, and pinch the edges together. Brush with the beaten egg yolk to glaze and prick it all over with a fork to allow the steam to escape.

Bake the pie until the pastry is golden and cooked through, 20–30 minutes.

Lavash, chicken & herb pie with barberries

This extremely simple dish, taught to me by an Armenian friend, is one of the best ways to turn chicken leftovers into something mind-blowing – although it would be totally worth poaching a whole chicken just to make this. Herbs, seasoned yogurt, barberries, toasted sunflower seeds, chicken, crispy top – I can't think of anything better to eat on a Monday night. If you live alone, or like me with a small child, you can make a mini version using a smaller baking sheet.

Serves 6

6 tablespoons (3½ oz/100 g) Homemade Matsoni (page 29) or plain yogurt

2 garlic cloves, grated

pinch of saffron threads (optional)

a pinch of cayenne pepper

1 tablespoon dried barberries or golden raisins

generous 1 cup (7 oz/200 g) poached chicken meat, torn into chunks

1 tablespoon chopped green onions

1 tablespoon chopped cilantro

1 tablespoon chopped dill

1 tablespoon chopped tarragon

sea salt flakes

¼ cup (2 oz/50 g) unsalted butter, melted

1 large piece of Armenian or Persian lavash (or any other thin flatbread)

1 tablespoon sunflower seeds (or sesame, pumpkin, or linseed)

To make a filling, mix the yogurt, garlic, saffron, cayenne, and barberries together, then add the chicken, green onions, and herbs. Season well with salt and set aside.

Preheat the oven to 350°F (180°C). Grease a shallow 6 x 8–inch (15 x 20–cm) baking dish with some of the melted butter.

Place one layer of lavash in the dish (tear it to fit), brush with melted butter, then spread the filling over. Cover with another layer of lavash. Brush with melted butter and sprinkle with the seeds.

Bake until the pie is heated through, the top is golden, and the seeds are toasted, 15 minutes.

Tip In addition to being a perfect way in which to use up leftover cooked chicken, this is also a great way to use up stale flatbreads; because you cover them with butter and the filling is so moist, the flatbreads revive beautifully in the oven.

Khingal

We often perceive comfort food as something lovely yet also a little bland and unassuming. It may not blow our minds with flavor, but it gives us that feeling of safe satiety. When I tried *khingal* in the Azerbaijan capital Baku, it was a complete revelation to me. It did all those things that comfort food does, except it also made my eyes widen as my mouth was filled with firm pasta, crispy aromatic lamb, and milky, but also oh-so-fresh, sauce. And then there is the butter. Pasta, spice, butter, crispy meat bits, yogurt, herbs – this dish has every single component that makes me feel safe and yet also titillates my senses, what I imagine a perfect marriage may be like.

Serves 8

- 1 large egg, lightly beaten
- ¼ cup (2 fl oz/60 ml) water
- 1⅔ cups (7 oz/200 g) all-purpose flour, plus extra if needed and for dusting
- 6 tablespoons (3½ oz/100 g) Clarified Butter (page 53) or ¼ cup (2 oz/60 g) unsalted butter and 2 tablespoons vegetable oil, plus extra for cooking the onions
- 10 oz (300 g) coarsely ground lamb
- 1 teaspoon coriander seeds, lightly toasted and ground
- 1 teaspoon cumin seeds, lightly toasted and ground
- ½ teaspoon ground turmeric
- sea salt flakes and freshly ground black pepper
- 2 onions, thinly sliced
- ¾ cup (7 oz/200 g) plain yogurt
- 1 garlic clove, finely grated
- a little milk or water as needed
- 1 tablespoon chopped cilantro
- 1 tablespoon chopped dill
- ½ teaspoon ground sumac

To make a pasta dough, mix the egg and water together in a bowl, then gradually add the flour (stop if the mixture seems to be getting dry) and knead the mixture in the bowl into a dough. You should end up with a firm, elastic pasta dough, so knead in more flour if it feels too wet. Cover it in plastic wrap and leave to rest in the refrigerator for 15–30 minutes.

Preheat the oven to 325°F (160°C), ready for keeping the lamb and onions warm.

Heat half the clarified butter or half the ordinary butter and 1 tablespoon oil in a pan over high heat. When really hot, add half the ground lamb – you want the meat to be crispy, so overcrowding the pan is not an option here. Fry it without disturbing it too much until it starts crisping up. Add half the spices and some seasoning and cook for 1 minute, then pop into a heatproof bowl and keep warm in the oven.

continued »

Repeat with the second batch of meat.

Don't wipe out the frying pan but place over medium-low heat, add some more butter or oil, and cook the onions gently until they become deep golden and luscious. Be patient – it will be worth it. Season them, too, and add them to the lamb keeping warm in the oven.

Roll out the pasta, either by hand or using a pasta machine, but not too thin – about $\frac{1}{16}$ inch (2 mm) thick – as you want a little bit of a bite here. Then cut the pasta into $1\frac{1}{4}$-inch (3-cm) diamonds. You can let them dry out slightly while you rustle up the yogurt sauce.

You can leave this sauce simple – just mix the yogurt with the garlic and a tiny bit of salt, adding a little milk or water to loosen it up. I also like adding the chopped cilantro and dill to it, as well as dusting the whole dish with sumac at the end.

Bring a large saucepan of salted water to a boil and drop in your pasta diamonds. They will be ready within 2 minutes. Check that they are cooked by tasting one when they float to the top. Drain them quickly and layer with the meat and onions, drizzling over the yogurt sauce as you go. Serve hot.

Tip *Sometimes I stir a little bit of brown butter (see page 80) into the yogurt. Don't judge me.*

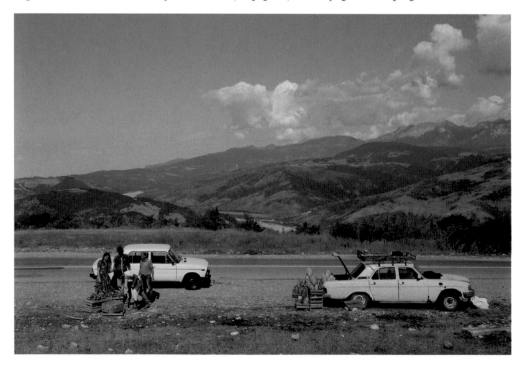

Zeti's kubdari or Svaneti meat pie

Tina is originally from the eastern Georgian region of Kakheti, but she met a Svaneti man, Amiran, and they then moved to Svaneti in the northwest. Tina is a village doctor and walks (she refuses to use a bike or horse) for about six miles every day to work. She also wakes up at 5 a.m. each day to milk the cows and does a million other things around the house. Her husband and their Russian friend Sergey, who's lived with them for the past 17 years, work hard on the land. Tina's mother-in-law Zeti taught her how to make this famous Svaneti dish. Hand-chopping the meat is very important here – ready-ground beef just won't have the same level of juiciness. If you don't have time to make the Svaneti salt, you can purchase it online.

Makes 3

FILLING
- 1¼ lb (550 g) boneless leg or neck of pork
- 2 mild onions, finely diced
- 3 garlic cloves, finely chopped
- 1 teaspoon red pepper flakes

SPICE MIX
- 2 tablespoons coriander seeds, ground
- 1 tablespoon ground blue fenugreek
- ½ teaspoon black peppercorns, freshly ground
- sea salt flakes or Svaneti Salt (page 63), to taste

- 1 recipe quantity of Adjaran Khachapouri dough (page 103)
- organic white bread flour, for dusting
- melted unsalted butter, for brushing

Using a very sharp knife (or a meat cleaver if you are comfortable using one), cut the pork into very thin strips and then cut the strips across. You should end up with very small pieces of meat. Combine with the rest of the filling ingredients and 1½ tablespoons of the spice mix.

Preheat the oven to 400°F (200°C).

Divide the dough into 3 pieces, 5 oz (150 g) each. Take each piece of dough and, using the back of your hand, stretch it into a thick 6-inch (15-cm) round. Place the same weight of filling (5 oz/150 g) on each round and spread it out. Bring the edges of the dough up over the meat, pleating as you go, and pinch the ends together really well at the top to secure it like a money bag. Start flattening the pouch out again with your hands, then sprinkle a little flour over the top and flip it over. Stretch the dough out again with the back of your hand into a 10-inch (25-cm) round.

Transfer to large baking sheets and cook in the oven for 15 minutes (you may need to do this in batches). Brush each with some melted butter as soon as it comes out of the oven.

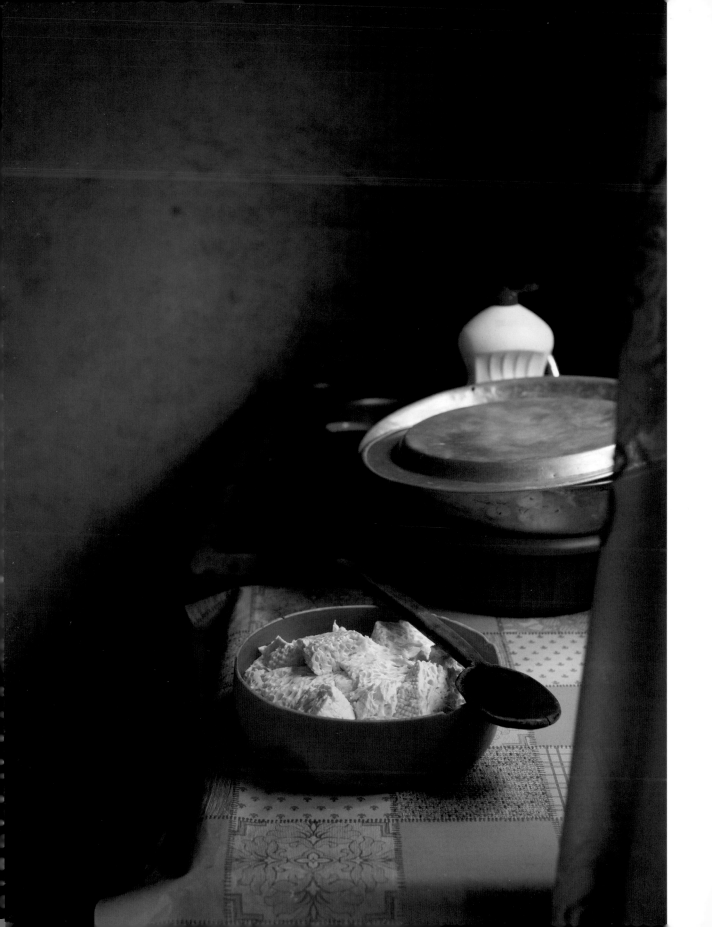

Fresh homemade cheese

In Georgia, a lot of people make this cheese every day. The cheese can either be eaten fresh on the day of making – it's wonderful on toast with Mint Adjika (page 25) – or left to ripen for a couple of days in the kitchen until it develops large holes. It is then fit for making the salty stretchy cheese known as *sulgun* in Svaneti, or *suluguni* in the rest of Georgia (see page 108). The drained whey shouldn't go to waste, as it can be used instead of *matsoni* for making bread (see page 29) or, in Tina's case, for feeding her pregnant pig! This is a fun project, and not too difficult.

Makes 14 oz–1⅓ lb (400–600 g)
- 1 gallon (4 qt/4 L) raw milk
- 12 teaspoons liquid rennet (or according to the bottle instructions)

TO SERVE
- crushed toasted coriander seeds or red pepper flakes (optional)

You will also need a piece of cheesecloth pressed with a hot iron to sterilize it

Heat the milk in a large saucepan until it is just comfortably warm (like in the cow's udder, Tina tells me). The ideal temperature is 86–104°F (30–40°C) – at 140°F (60°C); it will not be able to curdle, so make sure you don't overheat it.

Add the rennet and stir the mixture for about a minute to make sure the rennet is thoroughly incorporated. Then leave to stand for about an hour until you have what cheesemakers call a "clean break," where you can hook your forefinger through the set curds and they feel firm, the whey fills the gap, and there are few or no curds left on your finger.

The curds should by now separate from the whey. Cut the curds with a balloon whisk a few times and then leave to rest for 20 minutes before scooping out the curds with a slotted spoon. The idea is to increase the surface area of the curds to release more whey, which produces a drier cheese.

Line a fine-mesh sieve with the cheesecloth, add the cheese, and leave to drain over a bowl overnight in the refrigerator. Remove the cheese from the refrigerator and reserve the drained whey for making bread or homemade rennet, or give it to a pregnant pig.

Left in your kitchen at 77°F (25°C), the cheese will ripen and can be used the next day; if the temp is higher, you can make the fresh cheese in the morning and in the evening it will be ready for making *suluguni* (see page 108). Serve with the coriander seeds or red pepper flakes, if you like.

Mum always laughs about what she calls Georgian "greyhound pigs," long-legged and lean, left to roam free, splashing in puddles. Despite animals being everywhere (in western Georgia the cow owns the road), we did not sample many meat dishes while travelling through Georgia and Azerbaijan. Of course, meat is easily available, but people who take care of their own pigs and cows rarely eat meat – only when the season is right. This is what my grandparents did in Ukraine. Meat was a rarity, a luxury, which is what it is supposed to be in my opinion. I still live by these rules, eating mostly vegetables, and, if indulging in meat, eating head to tail (I will never sniff at giblets or tails). I buy meat of the highest quality, which guarantees the animal had a good life. I think they call it "flexitarian" these days. I call it "way of life as it should be, and now more than ever."

beasts from land, sea & air

Chicken chigyrtma

There are so many ways to extract flavor from saffron. Some advise pouring hot water over it; some say to grind it with salt with a mortar and pestle. My friend Zulya instructed me to soak it in a bowl of warm water (hot water kills the flavor, she says), with the bowl standing on a warm surface.

Serves 6–8

6 tablespoons (3½ oz/100 g) Clarified Butter (page 53)

1 small organic chicken, cut into 10 pieces

4–5 onions, not too thinly sliced

pinch of ground turmeric

pinch of saffron threads, soaked in ¼ cup (2 fl oz/50 ml) warm water for 5 minutes with the bowl standing on a warm surface

¼ cup (2 fl oz/50 ml) verjuice or lemon juice

1 tablespoon granulated sugar

6 eggs

1 tablespoon plain yogurt

Saffron Plov (page 120), to serve; Zulya's Plov Condiment (page 121); and any other dishes you like such as Pickled Cherries & the Gang (page 186)

Heat the clarified butter in a large pan over medium-high heat and brown the chicken pieces, in batches, really well. Set aside.

Add the onions to the pan and fry over medium heat until they are light golden, about 10 minutes, then stir in the turmeric, the saffron and its soaking water, verjuice, and sugar.

Return all the chicken to the pan, cover with a lid, and cook for 10–15 minutes. Then turn off the heat and leave to cool.

Preheat the oven to 350°F (180°C).

Beat the eggs and yogurt together.

Pack the chicken and onions snugly into a baking dish and pour the egg mixture over, then prod all over with a spoon so that the egg mixture is evenly distributed. Bake until golden and crispy on top, 35 minutes, then serve as part of a bigger feast.

Nazilya's cholme kiabab

Zulfiya's Aunt Nazilya from Lankaran is the most incredible cook. She uses a gorgeous plum and walnut stuffing for both fish and chicken – this one is a real classic. This is originally a broiled dish, as whole birds are often cooked in *tandyr* (tandoori-style) ovens in Azerbaijan.

Serves 4–6

1 small organic chicken

2 tablespoons Alycha paste (*tursha*) or tamarind paste (any tart, fruity paste will do)

sea salt flakes

1 recipe quantity of Fish Lavangi Winter Filling (page 160)

Rub the chicken with the Alycha paste, season with some salt, then stuff the cavity with the *lavangi* filling, spreading some all over the chicken. You may need to secure the cavity with a couple of toothpicks so that the filling doesn't spill out.

Pop the chicken breast side down into a large pan and add 6 tablespoons (3 fl oz/100 ml) water. Cover the pan with a lid and cook over a gentle heat for an hour, turning the bird over halfway through. The liquid should have reduced into a sticky, slightly tart, and flavorsome sauce.

Vine leaf dolmas

I tried this recipe using a mysterious preserved leaf I found at a market in Baku. The woman assured me that what I was buying was *lipa*, or linden tree leaves, but I think they were actually young quince leaves. I was surprised to discover how many different leaves can be used for stuffing, although the more easily available vine leaves are fine to use here.

Makes 28

2 tablespoons vegetable oil

2 large onions, finely diced

½ carrot, scrubbed and roughly grated

1 tablespoon chopped cilantro

1 tablespoon chopped mint

1 tablespoon chopped dill

2 teaspoons ground cumin

2 teaspoons ground coriander

1 teaspoon fennel seeds, toasted and ground

1 lb (400 g) boneless, fatty cut of beef and 1 lb (400 g) skinless pork belly, coarsely ground together (ask your butcher to prepare)

1 cup (7 oz/200 g) basmati rice, parboiled and cooled

sea salt flakes and freshly ground black pepper

10 oz (300 g) fresh vine leaves or 1 lb (500 g) preserved

2 cups (16 fl oz/500 ml) chicken or other meat or vegetable stock

plain yogurt, seasoned with a tiny bit of crushed garlic, a pinch of ground cinnamon, and salt, to serve

Heat the oil in a large frying pan, add the onions, and cook gently until they soften and start becoming golden, about 15 minutes. Add the grated carrot and cook over higher heat, stirring from time to time, until that, too, begins to caramelize, 3–5 minutes. Add the herbs and spices and cook over medium heat for a further minute.

Leave the vegetable mixture to cool, then mix it with the ground meat and the rice. Season with salt and pepper.

Blanch the vine leaves – the fresh ones only need to see the water for 10 seconds or so; the preserved leaves 2 minutes.

Go through the vine leaves, and if there are some that are damaged or seem too tough, don't throw them away but layer them over the base of a flameproof casserole dish that you will be cooking your dolmas in.

To assemble the dolmas, lay the first vine leaf for stuffing in front of you on your work surface, rough side up and shiny side down, with the point of the leaf facing away from you.

continued »

Take a tablespoon of the meat mixture and place it at the base of the leaf. Fold the right side of the leaf in over the meat mixture, then do the same with the left side. Starting from the base, roll up the leaf. Repeat with the rest of the vine leaves and meat, tucking the rolls next to each other in the casserole dish. You might get two layers out of them, depending on the size of your casserole.

Pour the stock over the dolmas and cover with a plate or something a little smaller in diameter than the casserole dish, then add a heavy weight on top, such as a can. The dolmas should be submerged in the stock, but there should be about ¾ inch (2 cm) of space left above in the pan so that the bubbling stock doesn't escape from the pan.

Cook the dolmas over low heat, uncovered, for about 1¼ hours. If there is still a lot of liquid left once the cooking time is up, turn the heat up and cook until reduced. Serve the dolmas warm with some of the reduced pan juice drizzled over, along with the seasoned yogurt.

VARIATION
I've tried this recipe with interesting grains, like *siyez* wheat and *freekeh*. Just use them in exactly the same way as the rice.

Summer filling

2 tablespoons vegetable oil

2 onions, finely diced

½ carrot, scrubbed and roughly grated

½ bunch of tarragon, chopped

½ bunch of dill, chopped

½ bunch of mint, chopped

2 tablespoons chopped basil

1 tablespoon chopped cilantro

1 tablespoon chopped flat-leaf parsley

1 teaspoon dried mint

½ bunch of green onions, finely diced

1¾ lb (800 g) fatty ground lamb

1 cup (7 oz/200 g) rice, parboiled, well drained and cooled

10 oz (300 g) fresh vine leaves or 1 lb (500 g) preserved

2 cups (16 fl oz/500 ml) chicken or other meat or vegetable stock

sea salt flakes and freshly ground black pepper

Follow the method above, adding the green onions with the herbs.

Kharcho

Ia, the school head teacher in Megrelia (Samegrelo), taught me how to make the real-deal *kharcho*. It is not a soup but a hearty stew in western Georgia, so delicious I could drink the sauce on its own. Ia says that the original version was always made with chicken, but since it has become so popular around Georgia beef has been used, and as the beef version is considered better, it has become the go-to meat to use for this dish. They serve it with *gomi* (Georgian polenta) in Samegrelo, but it would be equally nice with polenta, plain rice, or any other carb you love.

Serves 4–6

- 2¼ lb (1 kg) beef shin or any other fatty beef, cut into large chunks
- 3 onions, roughly chopped
- 1 bunch of cilantro, leaves, stalks, and roots (if the latter are available, well washed)
- 1½ cups (5 oz/150 g) good-quality walnuts
- 2 tablespoons Red Adjika Salt (page 62; or see Tip below) or chile paste
- 2 teaspoons ground blue fenugreek
- 1½ tablespoons tomato paste
- 3 large garlic cloves, crushed
- a few pomegranate seeds (optional)

Put the meat into a saucepan and pour over enough cold water to cover by 2 inches (5 cm). Cook over the lowest heat possible for about 1½ hours, skimming off the scum from time to time. It should start becoming soft, ready to fall apart but not quite.

Meanwhile, blitz the onions, cilantro stalks, and roots (reserve the leaves), walnuts, *adjika* salt (or chile paste), and blue fenugreek in a blender or food processor.

Skim a little bit of the fat off the beef stock and spoon it into a small saucepan. Stir in the tomato paste and cook for 2 minutes, then add the onion and walnut paste. Cook over low heat for about 15 minutes, stirring often. If it becomes too dry, keep adding more beef fat.

Remove the meat from the stock and pull it off the bone. Increase the heat under the stock and reduce it to about 1⅔ cups (13 fl oz/400 ml). Add the pulled meat back into the stock, reduce the heat, and add the onion and walnut paste. Taste, and if you used the red *adjika* salt you may not need more salt. But add more if it needs it. Add the crushed garlic and cook for 1 minute.

Chop some of the cilantro leaves roughly and serve sprinkled on top. A few pomegranate seeds would also be nice if you have some.

Tip *Having the heat of red* adjika *salt here is quite important. But if you can't find or make it, whip up this alternative. Blitz 2 long red chiles with 5 peeled garlic cloves, 1 teaspoon coriander seeds, and 1 tablespoon sea salt flakes in a blender or food processor. Use in moderation, as this is essentially a wet flavored salt.*

Shakh plov

It never ceases to surprise me how far and wide Yotam Ottolenghi's influence has reached all around the world. Zulya is a big admirer of his, and she told me that her outstanding version of (generally much simpler) Shakh Plov was inspired by Ottolenghi's quinoa and rice pilaf recipe. This is a regal dish, fit for a prince – or your dinner party guests. Cut into the sonorously crunchy lavash crust at the table and let the jewelled filling spill out onto a platter. It is actually relatively easy to make, but it will look like you have been slaving all day to produce something this beautiful. This is a meal in itself, so simply serve with a few bunches of soft herbs like mint, dill, cilantro, and purple basil along with some flavorsome sliced cucumbers and tomatoes in the summer, or with pickled vegetables in winter (see pages 179–186). Do play around with the filling, too – you can use slow-cooked and gently spiced shredded lamb instead of chicken, or make it vegetarian by substituting briefly roasted squash for the meat.

Serves 6–8

1⅓ cups (10½ oz/300 g) Clarified Butter (page 53)

1¾ lb (800 g) boneless, skinless organic chicken thighs

good pinch of saffron threads

8 oz (200 g) banana shallots, sliced

sea salt flakes and freshly ground black pepper

1 teaspoon cumin seeds, lightly toasted and ground

⅞ cup (3 oz/80 g) sliced almonds, lightly toasted

½ cup (1¾ oz/50 g) dried sour cherries or dried barberries, or a mixture of both

¼ cup (1 oz/30 g) dried apricots, sliced

3 tablespoons (1 oz/30 g) golden raisins

1¾ cups (12 oz/350 g) premium basmati rice, soaked in heavily salted cold water for 2 hours and rinsed well

fifteen 8-inch (20-cm) thin lavash flatbreads

You will also need a deep ovenproof pan 10½–11 inches (26–28 cm) in diameter with a lid

Heat 1 tablespoon of the clarified butter in a large frying pan over medium-high heat and cook the chicken thighs, in batches, until golden all over but not necessarily cooked through. Set the chicken aside, but don't worry about cleaning the pan, as you will be cooking the shallots in it.

To prepare the saffron, add to ¼ cup (2 fl oz/50 ml) cold water in a bowl and leave to stand on a warm surface – they are cautious with saffron in Azerbaijan, believing that soaking it in hot water kills its flavor.

Melt a few more tablespoons of the clarified butter in the frying pan over medium heat and cook the shallots until soft and lightly caramelized.

Shred the chicken, then add it to the caramelized shallots with the saffron and its soaking water, and season well with salt and pepper. Stir in the cumin, sliced almonds, and dried fruit, then cover the pan with a lid and cook over low heat for 5 minutes. Turn off the heat and leave it to cool down a bit.

Meanwhile, fill a large pan with water, add loads of salt, and bring to a rolling boil. Add the rice to the boiling water, then wait for it to boil furiously, stirring once. Boil until al dente, 7 minutes, then drain it thoroughly. They use massive colanders in Azerbaijan with a surface area large enough to allow the rice to cool down properly, but instead you can tip the drained rice onto a large baking sheet and spread it out so that the steam escapes and the rice doesn't overcook.

Preheat the oven to 350°F (180°C).

Brush most of the lavash, one by one, with the remaining melted clarified butter – or dip into the butter in a bowl, as they do in Azerbaijan(!), then use to line the base and sides of the deep ovenproof pan, allowing enough overhanging the sides to cover the top when folded over. Build up 3 layers of the lavash with no holes showing, using your judgement as to how many lavash you want to dip into the butter, as you want it all to be buttery but not completely soaking.

Using a large spoon, add the chicken mixture to the lavash pan and then add the rice mixture gently so that it's not tightly packed in. Carefully fold the overhanging lavash over the rice to encase it.

Cover the pan with the lid and bake for 40 minutes. Then lower the oven temperature to 325°F (160°C), remove the lid, and bake for a further 10 minutes so that the top crisps up.

Using a thick kitchen towel, very carefully (as some butter might splatter you) tip the *plov* onto a platter. You should have something that looks like a gorgeous, crispy-skinned pie. Leave it to stand for 5 minutes before cutting it. You should hear a very satisfying crunchy sound.

Quince stuffed with lamb & caramelized shallots

Dolmas come in so many forms. In fact, anything stuffed with a bit of meat and rice can actually be called dolma, or *tolma* in Armenian, including eggplants, peppers, tomatoes, potatoes, vine leaves, quince leaves (!), and quince itself. To me, quince is the queen of fruit. Astringent, tannic, and sour when raw (try thin, raw slices sprinkled with salt and sumac), it becomes the most luxurious-tasting aromatic thing when cooked. And despite being very sweet, it lends itself so naturally to savory fillings. Look for it in Turkish shops come the autumn, and do not give this dish a miss. Serve it with a simple endive and pomegranate salad.

Serves 2

- 4 ripe quinces
- 2 tablespoons olive oil
- sea salt flakes and freshly ground black pepper
- 1 lb (400 g) coarsely ground lamb
- 2 teaspoons coriander seeds, toasted and crushed
- 2 teaspoons fennel seeds, toasted and crushed
- 2 teaspoons cumin seeds, toasted and crushed
- 1 tablespoon unsalted butter
- 6 shallots, sliced

Preheat the oven to 400°F (200°C).

Slice the quinces in half lengthwise and remove the cores, scooping out quite a bit of the flesh in order to be able to fit in the lamb.

Place the quince halves cut side up on a baking sheet. Drizzle over and rub in 1 tablespoon of the oil and sprinkle over some salt and a little pepper. Cover with foil and bake for 30 minutes.

Meanwhile, heat the other tablespoon of oil in a frying pan over high heat and fry the lamb for a few minutes along with the spices and some salt and pepper. Take the meat out and set aside.

Add the butter and the shallots to the pan, lower the heat, and cook them slowly until they soften and start turning golden. This can take up to 15 minutes.

Remove the foil from the quince and bake for a further 15 minutes.

Stuff the baked quinces with the lamb mixture and top with the shallots. Return to the oven until the quince is soft, about 10 minutes. Your house will be permeated with a sweet, warming aroma.

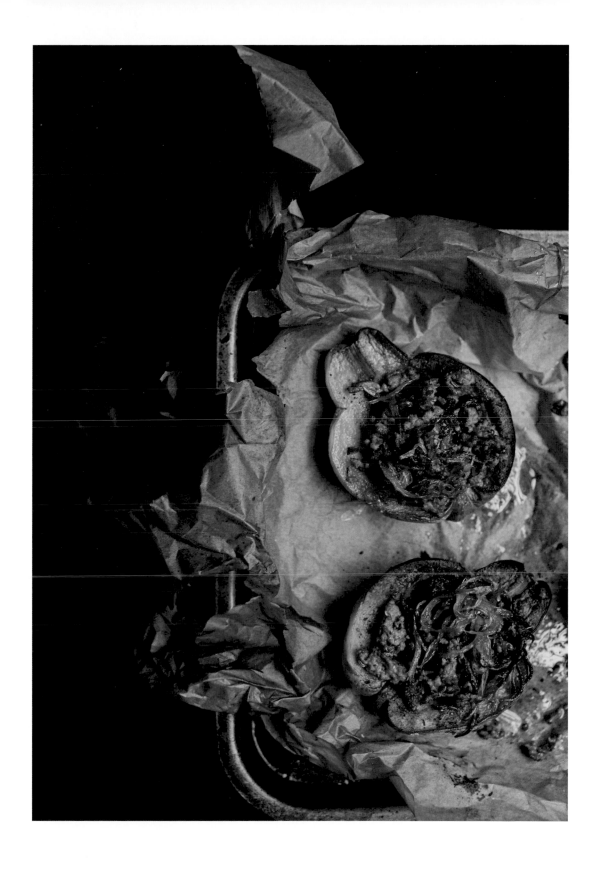

Poussin tabaka in blackberry sauce

Georgians love treating their fruit in a serious, savory way. Plums, grapes, mulberries – they all turn delectably savory with the addition of some garlic, salt, and strong soft herbs. Blackberries that are small and intense in flavor go really beautifully with chicken. In my first cookbook, *Mamushka*, I give the classic *tabaka* recipe and explain that the word *tabaka* comes from *tapa*, a special cast-iron pan traditionally used for cooking spatchcocked chickens, which were then covered in garlic oil. This recipe is the "next level" *tabaka*. You will experience savory fruitiness here in a new, thrilling, even mind-blowing way. Duck and its orange should take a break.

Serves 4

2 poussins (or 1 small organic chicken)

sea salt flakes and freshly ground black pepper

1 tablespoon vegetable oil

2 tablespoons unsalted butter

1 cup (4 oz/100 g) grapes

2½ cups (10 oz /300 g) blackberries

1 tablespoon verjuice or pomegranate molasses

2 garlic cloves, crushed

½ teaspoon cayenne pepper

1 teaspoon chopped marjoram or oregano

1 tablespoon chopped cilantro stalks

a tiny amount of dill

To spatchcock the birds, place each bird breast side down on a chopping board, and, using poultry shears or a sharp knife, cut along either side of the backbone. Then turn the bird over and flatten with the palm of your hand.

Season the birds very well with salt and pepper.

Heat the oil and butter in a large frying pan. Add the poussins cut side down and make sure you brown those bones, as this will add tons of flavor.

Now flip the birds cut side up and cook over medium-high heat for about 5 minutes to develop a bit of color. Cover with a cartouche (a circle of baking parchment or waxed paper), place another, slightly smaller frying pan on top, and then add a heavy weight, such as a can or heavy mortar and pestle. Cook over very low heat for 25 minutes.

Meanwhile, make the sauce. Blitz the grapes with the blackberries in a blender or food processor, or use a mortar and pestle if you want to be romantic about it, then pass through a sieve into a saucepan.

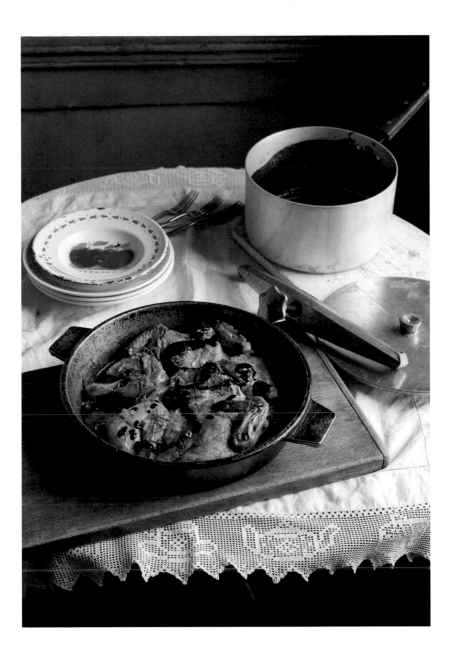

Add the verjuice and cook for a few minutes, then add the garlic, cayenne pepper, and marjoram and cook for a further 10 minutes. Finally, add the cilantro stalks to the sauce with the dill.

The poussins should be ready now, but check that the juices run clear when you pull at the legs. Take them out of the pan and leave to rest for a few minutes. You can mix the juices from the poussins through the sauce for extra lusciousness if you like. Pour the sauce over the birds and serve with a simple salad and a chunk of good bread.

Chicken satsivi

Both Ia and Nino make really special examples of *satsivi*, which I sampled in Georgia, so this recipe is the result of my taking the favorite bits from both. This is a festive dish, one that nobody would cook on an everyday basis because, even though walnuts grow in abundance in Georgia, they are expensive. I like to use this sauce as I would tahini. Turkey *satsivi* is a typical Christmas dish and it's a true wonder. As cooks, we are rarely faced with dealing with unplucked birds in the West, but this is how they would come in the Caucasus. On one occasion, Nino traveled with her dad from Baku to Tbilisi and they sat next to a couple of Azerbaijani women, live turkeys in hand. Conversation flowed and recipes were exchanged. What was particularly interesting, though, was the method that the women used to pluck their unfortunate birds. Instead of pouring boiling water on the skin, like Nino's mum used to do, they reported that they wrapped the (thankfully dead!) critters in wet cheesecloth and ran over them with an iron. Nino tried it the following Christmas and never looked back. It is equally effective with large game birds, apparently. But . . . maybe don't try this at home.

Serves 4–6

1 medium organic chicken, plus a bunch of chicken bones (ask your butcher)

sea salt flakes and freshly ground black pepper

2 small onions or 4 shallots, peeled and halved

vegetable oil, for oiling the chicken

2 cups (7 oz/200 g) dried walnuts (see Tip)

2 large garlic cloves, grated

1 teaspoon Red Adjika Salt (page 62) (optional)

½ tablespoon *khmeli-suneli* spice mix (see page 226)

1 teaspoon chopped cilantro

pinch of cayenne pepper

Put the chicken bones and a small pinch of salt into a saucepan and add about 1 qt (1 liter) cold water or enough to just cover. If there is a little bit of loose fat on your chicken, add that as well. Cook over low heat until the liquid has reduced by half, to about 2 cups (16 fl oz/500 ml), which will take about an hour. At first, skim off the scum, but then keep skimming the fat that rises to the surface and reserve it.

Meanwhile, preheat the oven to 400°F (200°C).

Place the onion or shallot halves in a roasting pan with the reserved chicken fat, season well with salt, and roast until they become soft and slightly caramelized, 20–30 minutes. Remove from the oven.

Reduce the oven temperature to 350°F (180°C).

Place the chicken in a roasting pan and lightly oil and heavily season. Roast for an hour and then check that the juices at the thigh bones run clear. You will be serving the chicken at room temperature, so it needs to be very juicy and tender.

Strain the stock and reduce it down again over high heat until you are left with about ¾ cup (6 fl oz/200 ml) of liquid. Leave to cool.

To make the *satsivi* sauce, blitz your perfect (or not!) walnuts in a blender or food processor to a powder, then add the garlic, *adjika* salt, if using, *khmeli-suneli*, confit onions, cilantro, and cayenne. Pour in most of your stock and blitz to a thin sauce. Keep adding the stock, or water, as needed until you have a heavy cream–like consistency.

Carve the chicken and place it in a large bowl or a deep platter. In Georgia, they pour the sauce all over and serve the dish at room temperature. With an average toasting session taking a good 15 minutes, no wonder so many Georgian *supra* (see page 172) dishes are served cold!

Tips

The walnuts, whether fresh or dried, need to be the best you can find, flawless with no blemishes, as we are looking for an almost white sauce.

I scatter the dish with some pomegranate seeds in winter, or red currants if I dare to make it in summer, and a few herbs, but that's not traditional.

You can gently heat a little walnut oil and cayenne pepper and drizzle this over the sauce to serve.

Kuchmachi

Do not be scared of the gizzards here. Gizzards . . . lizards . . . it's the English word that makes them sound so unappealing. Gizzard is such a harsh term for something so deep and rich in flavor. It was actually the first piece of meat I gave my six-month-old son, and he was delighted to "gnaw" on it with his teething-yet-still-toothless mouth. If you are still scared, try this dish using just the hearts. What can be more appealing than eating a being's heart? Especially when it's smothered in ruby, tangy pomegranate sauce and sprinkled with hazelnut shards. This is a dish to be made for an adventurous lover or an anemic friend. Otherwise, save some of it unsauced and give it to an unsuspecting suffering baby. They would all appreciate it.

Serves 2

- 3 tablespoons vegetable oil
- 8 oz (200 g) chicken hearts, trimmed
- 8 oz (200 g) chicken gizzards, trimmed (trimmed weight)
- 1 large onion, sliced
- 1 large garlic clove, sliced
- ¼ cup (1 oz/30 g) hazelnuts or ⅓ cup (1 oz/30 g) walnuts, finely chopped
- ½ teaspoon coriander seeds, toasted and ground
- ¼ teaspoon cayenne pepper
- ½ teaspoon dried wild thyme or za'atar herb (optional)
- 1 teaspoon pomegranate molasses
- sea salt flakes and freshly ground black pepper
- seeds of ¼ pomegranate

Heat 2 tablespoons of the oil in a frying pan until very hot. Add the hearts and gizzards and leave them to cook until caramelized, meaning that it's important not to stir them too often, about 2 minutes on each side. When a lovely golden crust has formed, take them out of the pan.

Add the remaining tablespoon of oil to the pan and then the onion and cook over medium-low heat until softened and started to turn golden, 10–15 minutes. Add the garlic, nuts, spices, and thyme and cook for a further 5 minutes.

Return the meat to the pan, add the pomegranate molasses and a splash of water, season well with salt and pepper, then cover with a lid and cook over low heat for 20–30 minutes, or until the meat is as soft as you like it (I don't mind it being a tiny bit chewy, so I only cook it for 15 minutes).

Stir through the pomegranate seeds and serve with some rice or bread.

Tips

You can also add some chicken livers – fry them in the pan with everything else, but only add them back in to braise for the last 5 minutes of the cooking time so that they don't become dry and chalky, unless you don't mind dry and chalky, like me, in which case just add them with the hearts and gizzards.

If you have leftovers, this is delicious used as a qutab filling (see page 87).

Chakhapuli

This dish screams spring. A young lamb would be slowly cooked in the tenderest, youngest spring herbs. In Akhaltsikhe in southern Georgia, I've been told, this is made outside for a picnic of sorts by the river. The next morning, men would demand to drink the remainder of the juices to cure their sore heads. In Kakheti in eastern Georgia, where the dish is claimed to be from, a local chef told me that this was nonsense because, first of all, there simply wouldn't be any leftovers, he insisted bemused, and secondly, Kakhetian wine is so superior that a hangover is definitely not in the cards. Whatever each region's vibe, this dish is indeed the most delicious ode to spring there is. If you can't find sour plums, add a little verjuice or lemon juice at the end or some good-quality vinegar – I like to add tarragon white wine vinegar to intensify the flavor.

Serves 4–6

4½ lb (2 kg) very young lean lamb ribs (bone-in) or 3¼ lb (1.5 kg) boneless lamb neck

2 teaspoons coriander seeds, toasted and crushed

2 teaspoons ground blue fenugreek

¼ teaspoon cayenne pepper or 1 teaspoon Red Adjika Salt (page 62)

1½ cups (12 fl oz/350 ml) white wine

2 bunches of tarragon, leaves picked and roughly chopped

1 bunch of mint, stalks and all, roughly chopped

1 bunch of cilantro, stalks and all, roughly chopped

2 bunches of green onions, roughly chopped

10 garlic cloves, 8 roughly chopped, 2 crushed

sea salt flakes

handful of sour Alycha plums (or greengages), pitted and chopped, or 1 tablespoon verjuice or lemon juice or good-quality wine vinegar

dash of pomegranate molasses (optional)

Heat a large, heavy-bottomed flameproof casserole dish over medium-low heat. Holding the meat with tongs, cook the pieces, fat side down, to render the fat and brown it. If your lamb is fatty, tip the extra fat out.

Add all the spices and cook for a further minute, stirring.

Pour in the wine and let it boil for a minute.

Add half the herbs, all the green onions, and the roughly chopped garlic; season with salt and cover loosely with a lid. Cook for about an hour over a very low heat.

Stir in the sour plums, if available, and cook for 30–60 minutes – you are looking for the meat to be very tender and start to fall off the bone.

When almost ready, add the rest of the herbs and the crushed garlic, along with the verjuice, lemon juice, or vinegar if you haven't added the sour plums. Sometimes I also add a dash of pomegranate molasses at this stage. Give it all a good mix, season to taste with salt, and serve with some good crusty bread or plain rice.

VARIATION

If stewing lamb is not to your taste, especially if you can't find a young, lean animal, you can do a slow-roast version of this. Simply blitz half the herbs with all the garlic and a couple of preserved lemons in a blender or food processor, mix in the spices and cover a shoulder or leg of lamb (I'd use a shoulder) in it. Cover with foil and roast in a preheated oven at 325°F (160°C), until it is soft and falls apart, 4–5 hours. Then turn up the oven to 425°F (220°C), remove the foil, and roast for a further 10 minutes so that the lamb browns well. Serve with some fresh herbs sprinkled all over it.

Tursh kiabab

This is not a kebab as we know it in the West. *Kiabab* in Azerbaijani does indeed mean "kebab" in English, and in the past the meat for this dish may well have been cooked over fire, but it's not in this version. And *tursh* simply means "sour." This is slow-cooked herby deliciousness – using the juice from the blitzed-up herbs was a real discovery. So was serving tender slow-cooked meat together with meatballs. And the eggplants here are a gorgeous slippery addition, not unlike snails in the best possible sense. When Zulfiya, who shared this recipe with me, tried snails in a chichi restaurant in Paris in 2004, she closed her eyes and exclaimed, "This tastes exactly like our Lankaran *tursh kiabab*!" Everybody laughed – she had a point. The amount of butter, garlic, parsley, and lemon in this beautiful dish is not far off that served with excellent escargots.

Serves 6

4½ lb (2 kg) leg of mutton on the bone, 1½ lb (700 g) chopped into cubes, the rest ground – ask your butcher to do this for you

1 onion, roughly chopped

2¼ cups (2½ oz/70 g) flat-leaf parsley, plus an extra 6½ cups (7 oz/200 g)

3 garlic cloves, plus 4 garlic cloves, peeled

⅔ cup (5 oz/150 g) Clarified Butter (page 53), plus extra for frying the eggplants

sea salt flakes and freshly ground black pepper

6 tablespoons (3 fl oz/100 ml) verjuice or juice of 2 lemons

dash of white wine vinegar

10 baby eggplants or 2 large

Mix the ground mutton with the onion, 2¼ cups (2½ oz/70 g) of the parsley, and the 3 garlic cloves, or blitz in a food processor. Cover and chill in the refrigerator for a couple of hours.

Heat ¼ cup (1¾ oz/50 g) of the clarified butter in a cast-iron pan over high heat and fry the meat cubes until thoroughly caramelized. Add enough water to cover the meat, bring to a boil, and skim off the scum, then lower the heat, cover the pan with a lid, and cook over very low heat until the meat is falling apart, about 1 hour. Make sure that the water doesn't evaporate completely, as you will need this stock. Season the meat with salt and pepper and the verjuice.

Blitz the remaining 4 garlic cloves with the remaining 6½ cups (7 oz/200 g) parsley in a blender or food processor, then squeeze out the juice, but don't throw it away. Mix half the blitzed herb mixture with the ground meat mixture, and season well with salt and pepper.

Heat the remaining 6 tablespoons (3½ oz/100 g) clarified butter in a large pan over medium heat and fry the rest of the blitzed parsley and garlic until the herbs are dry but not burnt.

Mix the vinegar and some salt into a bowl of water and use to wet your hands before you shape the ground meat mixture into marble-sized meatballs (wetting your hands makes this easier), then place in the refrigerator.

If using baby eggplants, fry them whole in a little clarified butter until golden all over. If using large eggplants, slice them into ¾-inch (2-cm) rounds before frying.

Add the fried parsley and garlic to the lamb stock and bring it to a boil, then very gently drop the meatballs into the stock. Now add the herb juice, lower the heat to its minimum, cover with a lid, and cook for 30 minutes.

Add the eggplants to the pan, check for seasoning, and cook for a further 15 minutes. Serve with Shakh Plov (page 128) and plain yogurt or Homemade Matsoni (page 29).

VARIATION
You can use a few tablespoons of vegetable oil instead of the Clarified Butter for cooking the blitzed parsley and garlic, but the flavor will be different.

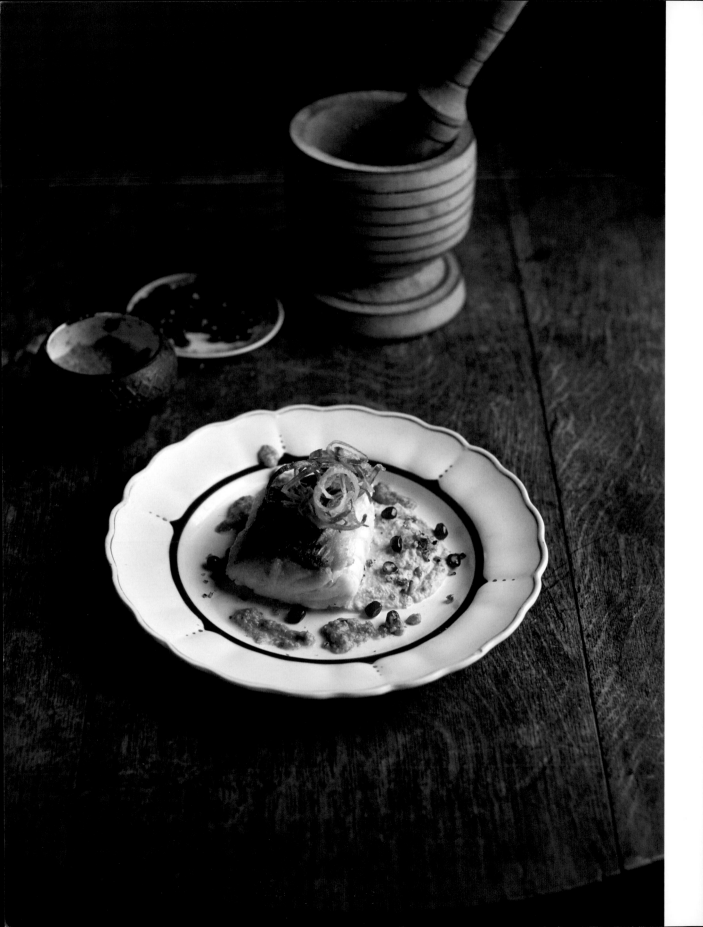

Fish with pistachio & cauliflower sauce & kindzmari

This dish came out of the numerous Georgian supper clubs I have staged in the UK. I love the creaminess of Georgian nut sauces like *satsivi* (see pages 136–7), but also the acidity and aroma of *kindzmari*, so this is a great way to enjoy a bit of both. If you are cooking for a dinner party and want to dress it up in style, you can also add something crispy on top as I've suggested below. If you want to simplify the recipe, simply drop one of the sauces – a good fish would be equally delicious with either a dollop of the nutty cauliflower mixture or a slick of *kindzmari* and some simple boiled potatoes, depending on whether your preference is for creamy comfort or a spicy kick. But if you do have the time and the will, this is not a difficult dish to prepare, especially if you aim to impress someone.

Serves 4

PISTACHIO & CAULIFLOWER SAUCE
   ½ small cauliflower, divided into florets
   2 shallots, peeled and halved
   2 tablespoons unsalted butter
   ¾ cup (6 fl oz/200 ml) warm chicken, fish, or vegetable stock
   sea salt flakes and freshly ground black pepper
   small pinch of saffron threads
   ½ cup (2½ oz/70 g) pistachios or walnuts, toasted

KINDZMARI
   1-oz (25-g) bunch of cilantro, stalks and all, roughly chopped
   2 green chiles, roughly chopped
   1 garlic clove, roughly chopped
   2 tablespoons white wine vinegar
   1 tablespoon maple syrup or clear honey
   sea salt flakes, to taste

   2 tablespoons vegetable oil
   4 hake fillets

TO SERVE (IF YOU WANT TO BE FANCY)
   floured and shallow-fried shallot rings (or toasted sliced almonds or crispy seaweed)
   herbs or micro leaves
   pomegranate seeds

To make the pistachio and cauliflower sauce, preheat the oven to 350°F (180°C). Pop the cauliflower florets and halved shallots onto a baking sheet, dot the butter around, and pour half the chicken stock over. Season well with salt. Crush the saffron with a little sea salt using a mortar and pestle and add that as well.

continued »

Roast the vegetables until the liquid has gone and they look soft and caramelized, about 30 minutes. If the cauliflower gets a little bit brown at the edges, it's not a problem, and the same applies to the shallots – you need them to have color for the sauce to be flavorsome.

Grind the pistachios in a powerful food processor (or use an electric spice or coffee grinder) into a powder. Then blitz the shallots and cauliflower with the ground nuts in a blender or food processor until the mixture is super smooth, adding some more of the warm stock if the mixture needs help to blend. It should be the consistency of heavy cream, but if your blender or processor is not strong enough to produce a completely smooth sauce, don't worry – it will still taste good. Taste and season some more if you feel that it's still under-seasoned.

To make the *kindzmari* sauce, blitz all the ingredients in (again!) a powerful blender or food processor. The resulting mixture should be quite liquid but smooth, without any bits of stalk, and the flavor should be primarily sour but also spicy and a tiny bit sweet. You can drop the maple syrup or honey for a more authentically tart version, but I like the hint of sweetness here. The sauce may turn a dark, muddy green, but who cares as long as it's delicious!

To cook the hake, preheat the oven to 400°F (200°C).

Heat the oil in a large frying pan with an ovenproof handle. Season the fish skin with salt and pop it down into the hot oil. After a minute, shake the pan gently so that the skin doesn't get stuck. Cook for 2 minutes, then flip the fish over and transfer the pan to the oven for a further 5–7 minutes (depending on the thickness of your fillet) to finish cooking it.

To serve the fancy way, put some slightly warmed cauliflower sauce on a plate, dot around a spoonful of *kindzmari* and then add the hot fish skin side up. Scatter with the shallots, almonds, or seaweed, the herbs, and/or the pomegranate seed garnish, if using.

VARIATIONS

I've used pistachios here because I love them, although walnuts would be more traditional, but I don't see a problem with using any nut you fancy and I struggle to find good walnuts in the UK – just use the best you can get hold of. Quality is what's important here.

A piece of expertly cooked pork fillet would not be out of place here instead of the fish. I have also made this using scallops, or if you want to go vegetarian, fry a cauliflower steak in some butter and a little oil until caramelized.

Fish lavangi

In the West, we are constantly told that meat must be really tender – heaven forbid that there be any resistance to the teeth, or any cartilage! We are also told that fish must only see the pan for a fleeting moment; otherwise, it will become dry and inedible. In many cases, yes indeed, braised meat is nicer if falling apart, or a steak if expertly cooked or fish if quickly roasted until it is only just cooked. But there is also room for slightly chewy gizzards, or slow-cooked liver that is no longer pink, or slightly chewy pork *mtsvadi*. We have teeth for a reason and not everything needs to melt in the mouth. In Lankaran in southeastern Azerbaijan, they love to cook fish slowly in a *tandyr* or outside clay oven, stuffed with a delicious juicy filling. Some may think that the flesh is a little drier than what is usually considered desirable, but I love how crispy the skin gets and I am fine with the texture of the fish, so I have not adapted this recipe to the Western palate. The stuffing has time to cook properly inside the fish, developing and exchanging flavors with its flesh. It is absolutely delicious and I urge you try it, especially in winter when walnuts are of the best quality. Not everyone has a *tandyr* oven in their backyard or garden, not even in Lankaran, so a frying pan and a lid are used, but you can also use the oven.

Serves 2

1 whole sea bream or red mullet, about 1½ lb (700 g), gutted and scaled

sea salt flakes and freshly ground black pepper

4 tablespoons Alycha paste (*tursha*) or soaked sour fruit leather (*lavashana*; see page 228) or tamarind paste

Summer Filling or Winter Filling (recipes follow)

2 tablespoons all-purpose flour, if frying

corn oil, if frying

You will also need a large, stout needle and thread

Slash the fish along the backbone and then rub with some salt and pepper and the Alycha paste or *lavashana* or tamarind paste all over the fish's skin.

Stuff the filling into the belly of the fish – it has to be pretty full and bulging – then grab your needle and thread and sew up the belly to enclose the filling.

Dust one side of the fish with the flour.

Heat some corn oil in a large frying pan over medium heat and fry the fish on the floured side for 2 minutes. Flip the fish, then cover the pan with a lid, lower the heat and cook for

continued »

about 30–40 minutes until the skin is well browned. Serve with some rice or Saffron Plov (page 120) with some cooked lentils stirred through.

Tip *In Azerbaijan, they use kutum, or Caspian roach, for this dish – a predator that feeds on crustaceans, so just imagine the resulting flavor of the fish! I have suggested sea bream as a more widely available option, or you can try red mullet instead, but feel free to choose the best sustainable fish you can find.*

Summer filling

handful of dried Alycha plums or dried sour cherries

2 red onions, peeled and finely chopped

1 green bell pepper, cored, seeded and finely chopped

1 red chile, finely chopped

½ bunch of mint, leaves picked and finely chopped

½ bunch of flat-leaf parsley, leaves picked and finely chopped

½ bunch of cilantro, leaves picked and finely chopped

½ bunch of purple basil, leaves picked and finely chopped

2 tomatoes, finely chopped

grated zest and juice of 1 lemon

sea salt flakes and freshly ground black pepper

Soak the dried Alycha plums or sour cherries in some warm water until they become plump, about 1 hour. Drain the dried fruit, then mix with the rest of the filling ingredients, seasoning well with salt and pepper, getting in there with your hands and massaging the ingredients together really well. Use as directed on previous page to stuff the fish.

Winter filling

1 lb (400 g) banana shallots, peeled

2 tablespoons Alycha paste (*tursha*) or handful of dried Alycha plums or blitzed dried sour cherries or tamarind paste

1 cup (3½ oz/100 g) walnuts, lightly toasted and ground into a powder

sea salt flakes and freshly ground black pepper

You will also need a piece of cheesecloth

Blitz the shallots in a blender or food processor, then enclose in the cheesecloth and squeeze out all the juice. You will end up with a handful of wrung-out shallot.

Mix the shallots with 2 tablespoons of the Alycha paste and all the other ingredients, seasoning well with salt and pepper. Use as directed on previous page to stuff the fish. (You can also freeze this mixture at this point for up to a month.)

Boy, do they know how to drink in Georgia. A *tamada*, or toastmaster, can easily kill twelve quarts of wine during a *supra*, a Georgian feast. Every toast (which is more of a poetical philosophical discussion) takes at least fifteen minutes, so there are long pauses. Pauses or none, it depends on how good the wine is. It isn't always perfect, so the next day a cure is needed, and Georgians know the best cures in Caucasus. Initially, I thought this would be the "hangover chapter," but actually this is a chapter for those who need nourishment. The broths here will cure a grown man's sore head as well as help a small child recover from a cold equally well.

pain, be gone!

Village breakfast

We often make a breakfast like this in Ukraine (it's my Aunt Lynda's specialty), and this is what I cooked up in Tbilisi for friends, which they loved, spiced up with a little chile. After all, Georgians are the great recipe adaptors (see *Ostriy*, page 144). It's a perfect dish for using up old bread, and although it's called breakfast, it also makes a great lunch or dinner – in fact, this is my universal go-to meal. The ingredients always include cured pork fat, bread, eggs, and tomatoes, but the rest depends on what I have in the refrigerator; dill and green chiles often figure. This is simply one of the best meals in the world.

Serves 2

1 large ripe tomato

2 garlic cloves, crushed with salt

1 oz (20 g) *lardo*, torn if in thin slices or finely chopped

4 small pieces of stale bread (sourdough, rye, or anything you like)

1 red or green chile, diced

4 eggs

sea salt flakes

½ tablespoon chopped dill

½ tablespoon chopped cilantro

½ tablespoon chopped basil

Slice the tomato across the equator into 4 rounds and spread a tiny smidgen of the crushed garlic over them.

Heat the *lardo* in a large frying pan over medium heat, and when it starts to melt and sizzle, add the bread. Cook on one side until it starts to soften, then flip the bread pieces over and cook for another minute. Prop the bread up against the insides of the pan to make room for the rest of the ingredients.

Add the tomato rounds to the pan, garlic side up, and throw in the chile. Make a little space for the eggs and crack them all around the bread and tomato rounds.

Cook until the whites are set but the yolks are still runny, 5–7 minutes. Sprinkle a little salt over the egg yolks, throw the chopped herbs over, and serve immediately.

Tomato scramble

I love egg yolks. Even though egg whites are erroneously considered healthier for you, I never finish eating the white of a fried egg – too rubbery, too bland. I do love scrambled eggs, though, and in particular the combination of scrambled egg and sweet tomato. They do this in Azerbaijan a lot, including my friend Zulya who leaves the egg yolks whole! When I heard this, I knew it would be my favorite scrambled egg dish. So here is the perfect version – egg whites scrambled with tomato, with the egg yolks remaining whole and glorious, ready for your bread! Serve this dish as part of a bigger feast.

Serves 2

   2 tablespoons unsalted butter

   2 garlic cloves, grated

   3 ripe, tasty tomatoes, grated (see Tip below)

   sea salt flakes

   a little granulated sugar, to taste, if needed

   4 eggs

   1 tablespoon chopped cilantro or any other soft herb, such as dill (optional)

   sourdough bread, to serve

Melt the butter in a frying pan over low heat, add the garlic, and cook, stirring from time to time, until the garlic starts smelling sweet, 3–5 minutes. Be careful not to burn it.

Stir in the tomato pulp and then season the mixture with salt. Taste it and add a little sugar if you think it needs it. Cook the tomatoes until reduced and quite dry, 5–10 minutes.

Now the fun part begins. Crack the 4 eggs into the pan and gently mix the whites into the tomato sauce, scrambling them, leaving the egg yolks intact. Keep scrambling the whites with the tomatoes gently over low heat until they have set to your liking and the yolks look sufficiently heated through.

Sprinkle some sea salt over the yolks and add the herbs, if using, then eat, squashing the egg yolks into some sourdough bread and wiping the plate clean with the bread at the end.

Tip *Slice each tomato in half and grate it over a coarse box grater. If the tomatoes are decent (I wouldn't recommend using anything else), don't throw away the skins but chop them finely and add it, too.*

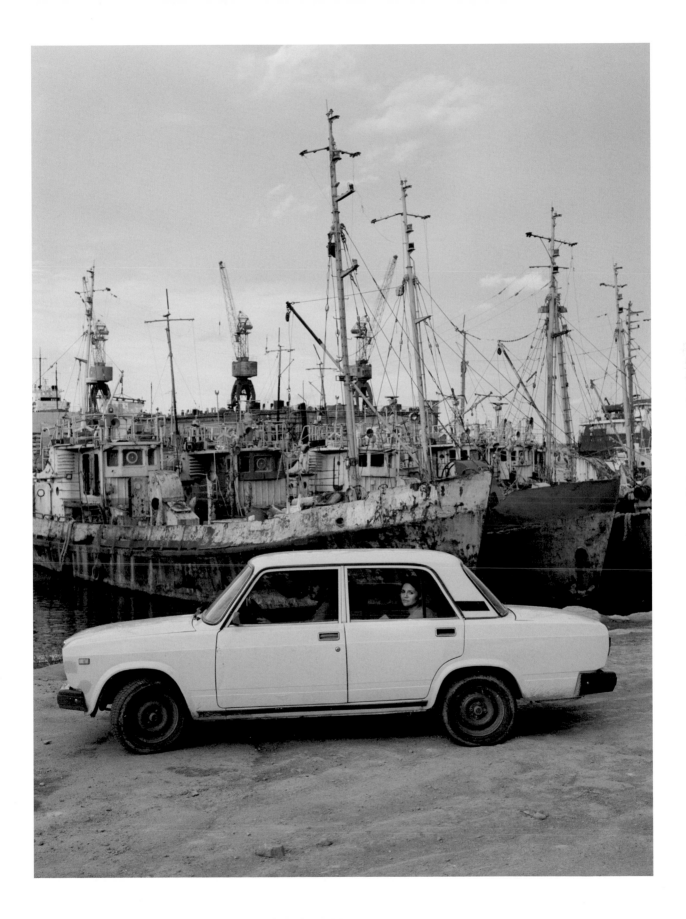

Khash

Stop gawping. This has nothing to do with charas or hashish, although its taste is as beautifully intoxicating. *Khash* is the ultimate hangover cure – a deeply meaty, thick broth, so simple, so genius. Pretty much every country in the Caucasus claims a right to its invention, but the point is, it doesn't really matter where it originated. I once had something very similar cooked for me by a Colombian friend's mum (called *caldo de costilla*, I believe), so this kind of dish is probably universal. I like the story of its origins in Georgia as a hangover cure – after a long, heavy night of feasting and drinking, a few large pieces of beef (and often some tripe) would be thrown into the pot before the revelers went to bed, and cooked slowly all night. In the early hours, woken by throbbing headaches, the men would get up, pour a bowl of the viscous, sweet broth, add some salt and garlic, eat it, go back to bed, and wake up again fresh as the morning dew . . . probably only to go and enjoy another day of partying. Nowadays, people visit *khasherias*, eateries that specialize in *khash*. I must constantly remind myself to explain what those places actually are when back in the West, as eyes widen awkwardly when I mention the word!

Serves 6

4½ lb (2 kg) good-quality beef shin or ribs

1 lb (500 g) tripe (order in advance from your butcher and ask them to prep it for you) (optional)

2 onions, peeled but left whole

2 fresh bay leaves, crumbled

TO SERVE

3 tablespoons chopped cilantro

3 tablespoons chopped dill

3 tablespoons chopped purple or green basil

10 garlic cloves, finely grated

sea salt flakes

freshly ground black pepper or red pepper flakes (optional)

Put the meat into a large pan, cover with cold water, and add the onions and bay, then bring to a boil over medium heat. Skim off the foam that forms just as the broth is about to boil, then reduce the heat to its lowest setting.

Cook the meat for a few hours until it is very tender and starts falling apart, adding a little water to the pan if it reduces too much, and remember to keep skimming off the scum.

When the stock is strong and the meat tender, it is time to serve it. Put the herbs, garlic, and salt into separate small *pialas* (small ceramic bowls) and encourage your hungover guests to help themselves and season the broth to their liking. Feel free to add plenty of freshly ground black pepper or red pepper flakes.

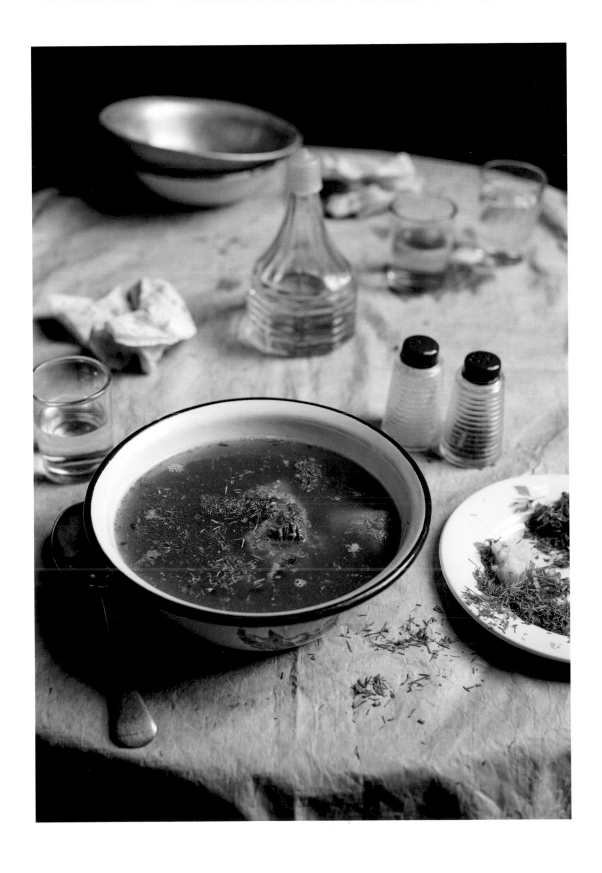

Poputsa's chikhirtma

Georgian men often name their daughters after the women who meant a lot to them. Nino's grandmother's real name was Ketevan, but Nino only knew her as Poputsa, a name that Nino's great-grandfather gave his little girl after his ex-beloved, who was also a famous Georgian writer. Before we took the photograph for this recipe (see pages 174–5), we were shown a lot of Poputsa's remarkable dowry – a rug she'd woven herself, an early twentieth-century tea set, and a stunning nineteenth-century Kuznetsov "dinner set." When Georgians have a *supra*, an elaborate, often all-night feast with much drinking and many a philosophical toast, the guests sometimes continue into the early hours with a morning *supra* – an after-party. If a hangover is already setting in, then *chikhirtma* is the soup of choice for some. It consists of a rich chicken stock, thickened with toasted flour and egg and spiked with vinegar, so rich and sharp at the same time. Served with a shot of *chacha* (Georgian grappa), this dish is eaten before going off to bed to slumber, only to wake up a few hours later refreshed and ready to repeat the feasting, especially if it's a special occasion like a wedding or a funeral.

Serves 6–8

2¼ lb (1 kg) boiling chicken
or 2 organic chicken carcasses

1 onion, peeled but left whole

2 carrots, scrubbed and roughly chopped

2 celery ribs, roughly chopped

5 black peppercorns

sea salt flakes

2 shallots, diced

1 tablespoon all-purpose flour

1 bunch of cilantro, leaves separated, stalks and well-washed roots (if the latter are available) chopped

pinch of saffron threads

3 egg yolks

2 tablespoons white wine vinegar

Place the chicken or chicken carcasses, onion, carrots, celery, peppercorns, and a pinch of salt in a 3-qt (3-liter) pan of cold water. Bring to a boil, then skim off the foam and lower the heat. Cook until the chicken is tender and the liquid has reduced by one-third, about 1 hour.

Skim 2–3 tablespoons of the chicken fat off the surface of the broth and pour it into a frying pan. Heat the fat, add the shallots, and cook gently until they start to caramelize ever so slightly, 5–10 minutes if you have the patience. Keep adding more skimmed chicken fat if the pan becomes too dry – it should have some moisture before adding the flour.

Add the flour and a touch more chicken fat and cook, stirring, for a few minutes to cook out the flour. Then add the cilantro stalks and roots and cook for about 5 minutes to soften.

Lift the chicken out of the broth and shred the meat into pieces – if you wish; it will make it easier to eat later.

Add the shallot and cilantro mixture to the broth. Grind the saffron with a little salt using a mortar and pestle, stir in a dash of the broth, and then pour the saffron liquid into the broth.

Whisk the egg yolks and vinegar together, then whisk into the gently simmering broth. Add the shredded chicken meat and cook for a few minutes, then serve scattered with the chopped cilantro leaves.

We accidentally spilled some wine at Nino's mum's place, meaning that her ancestors had given her the green light and welcomed us into their home.

Tarragon soup

Keti Sujashvili from Kazbegi in northeastern Georgia gave me this soup on a rainy June afternoon and I fell in love with it. When she told me the recipe, I knew it would be one of my very favorite ones in the entire book. It is so easy to make and won't take you longer than 30 minutes, but it packs a real punch of flavor. Once when I cooked this I forgot to add the rice and I didn't miss it, but do add it if you prefer thicker soups. If you use the eggs, they will add body to the soup, but add the eggs only if you're intending to eat it all on the day of cooking.

Serves 6

¼ cup (2 oz/50 g) unsalted butter

2 potatoes, peeled and roughly chopped

sea salt flakes

2 tablespoons mild olive oil

1 onion, diced

2 carrots, scrubbed and coarsely grated

2 bell peppers, 1 red and 1 green, cored, seeded, and sliced

2 large ripe tomatoes, grated (see Tip on page 167), skin discarded

⅓ cup (2½ oz/70 g) basmati rice (optional)

generous pinch of red pepper flakes

2 eggs, lightly beaten (optional)

2 small garlic cloves, finely grated

1 bunch of tarragon, leaves picked and chopped

Heat the butter in a saucepan over low heat, add the potatoes and coat them in the butter, then add 2 qt (2 L) water and a generous pinch of salt. Cook for about 5 minutes.

Heat the oil in a frying pan over medium heat, add the onion, and cook until soft and starting to go golden, about 7 minutes, then add the carrots and cook until they also start getting a little color, too, about 3 minutes.

Finally, add the peppers and sauté for a few minutes, then add the tomatoes. Keep stirring from time to time, so as not to let the mixture burn.

Add the sautéed vegetables, and the rice if using, to the potatoes and stock and cook until the rice and potatoes are tender, 10 minutes.

Lower the heat so that the stock is barely bubbling, add the red pepper flakes, and then gradually add the eggs, if using, whisking them in thoroughly.

Finally, whisk in the garlic, add the tarragon, and take the soup off the burner to serve.

Golnar's herb stalk broth

Ways of incorporating one's culture into a completely different environment can be really ingenious. Golnar, who was born in Germany but has grown up listening to her Azerbaijani grandmother's stories without ever having visited her homeland, had one of the strongest cultural and culinary longings I have ever seen in a person. The flavors of Azerbaijan and Persia are in her Berlin kitchen everywhere you look – spices, butter, dried fruit, and of course herbs. Fresh herbs, whole bunches of tarragon, dill, cilantro, wild garlic, and basil adorning the table, making almost a dish in themselves. In the morning, she took out a pot of incredibly flavorsome herb stock made from a bunch of herb stalks. The meatballs were rustled up in a few minutes, and some garlic and chopped dandelion (common in Berlin in April) were added to the broth at the end. It was one of the most delicious breakfasts I've had in a long time. Any bitter crunchy vegetable will do if cultivated dandelion is not common where you live. I have tried this with roughly chopped endive and Swiss chard, but absolutely anything will work.

Serves 4–6

10 oz (300 g) aromatic herb stalks, such as tarragon, cilantro, basil, and flat-leaf parsley, gently bruised (reserve some of the leaves for chopping to serve)

4 garlic cloves, 2 sliced, 2 crushed

sea salt flakes

8 oz (200 g) ground beef or lamb

small handful of dill

small handful of tarragon

2 tablespoons pomegranate molasses

3 dandelion stalks (or celery ribs, Belgian endive, or Swiss chard), roughly chopped

Put the whole herb stalks into 2 qt (2 L) cold water in a large pot, add the sliced garlic and some salt, and bring to a boil. Lower the heat and simmer for about 10 minutes. If you have time, leave the broth to cool and further infuse with the herb flavor. Strain the stalks out, but keep the stock.

Put the ground meat, some salt, and the dill and tarragon in a blender or food processor and blitz until well combined. Using slightly wet hands, form the meat mixture into small meatballs, about ½ inch (1 cm) across.

Bring the stock to a boil, add the meatballs and the pomegranate molasses, and cook until the meatballs are tender and cooked through, 5–8 minutes.

Finally, add the crushed garlic and dandelion stalks (or whatever crunchy stalks you have available) and cook for a further 2 minutes – you want them to remain fresh and still a little crunchy. Serve with a warm hunk of bread and the reserved chopped herb leaves.

Fermented jonjoli

Hallelujah! You can now get *jonjoli* (bladdernut buds) ready-fermented online (see page 234)! *Jonjoli*. It is gorgeous and it exists. But here is what you do should you come across some of the beautiful fresh clusters of white flower buds – or if you decide to move to Georgia! I hear it can be found in Italy and the Balkans too, although I always thought it was endemic to Georgia. Or try using the flower buds of the black locust tree if you can find some in your area (see page 228). They say to avoid washing the buds and to pick them after a spring rain (very romantic!).

Makes about 1 pint (16 fl oz/480 ml)

4½ lb (2 kg) jonjoli (bladdernut) flower bud clusters, shaken free of any insects

7 teaspoons (1½ oz/40 g) sea salt flakes

You will also need a sterilized 1-pint (16–fluid oz/480-ml) preserving jar, cheesecloth pressed with a hot iron to sterilize it, and a small ceramic or glass dish or jar that will fit inside the neck of the preserving jar

Pack the *jonjoli* into a sterilized plastic container, adding salt between the layers, and pressing down with your clean hands.

Cover the top of the container with a piece of the cheesecloth, then insert a small dish or something heavy to weight down the *jonjoli*.

Leave the container in your kitchen for a week or two (depending on temperature; if the temperature is warm, fermentation will begin more quickly than if it's cool) to start the fermentation process, cleaning and changing the cheesecloth every day.

Remove the cheesecloth and weight, transfer the contents into a jar, and pop it in the refrigerator. It should keep for a few months. You may need to rinse it before serving if it tastes too salty.

Pickled green chiles

Pickling and fermenting is a way of life in Georgia. Pickles come out in winter as often as they do in summer. From gorgeous and unique *jonjoli* (bladdernut) buds and fermented green tomatoes to these beautiful chiles, they stimulate the appetite and cut through the saltiness of dishes they are often served with.

Makes a 1½-qt (1.4-L) jar

3¼ lb (1.5 kg) long green chiles

1 qt (1 L) natural spring or still mineral water

3 teaspoons fine sea salt

2 tablespoons white wine vinegar or other good-quality mild vinegar

washed corn husks (see Tip below) or washed green parts of leeks or sturdy cabbage leaves

You will also need a sterilized 1½-qt (1.4-L) preserving jar and cheesecloth pressed with a hot iron to sterilize it

First we need to prep the chiles. This is a curious (for me) way of prepping and preserving chiles, but this is the recipe Nino gave me, and I am going with it. Leave your chiles out in your kitchen for a day so that they become a little softer.

On the second day, cut off the stems of the chiles and leave them out for another day.

Wash the chiles and drain them in a colander, then pack them tightly into the sterilized jar.

Put the water into a pan, add the salt, and heat gently, stirring, until dissolved, then leave to cool completely. Mix the cooled brine with the vinegar and pour it over the chiles.

Cover the jar with a piece of the cheesecloth and leave in your kitchen for about 3 days, cleaning and changing the cheesecloth every day.

Removing the cheesecloth, Nino then covers the chiles with the corn husks, which she says tint the chiles a lovely golden color and absorb some of the extra spice. If corn is out of season, I often use the green parts of leeks or some sturdy cabbage leaves. Seal the jar and store in a cool, dark place for up to a couple of months.

Tip Look for ears of corn still in their wrapping of leaves at markets or greengrocers from summertime into autumn.

Fermented green tomatoes

These are truly mind-blowing, delivering the strongest umami and chile kick you can imagine. You can eat them as they are, or chop them finely and serve with oysters. Or, use them to make a delicious relish to go with grilled meat or serve with some buttery, milky mashed potatoes. In fact, if you are hungover, ask your loved one to make you some luscious mash, then eat just that, gentle and creamy potatoes that don't require you to even chew, along with these tomatoes, so savory and sour, salty and firm.

Makes a 5½-qt (5.5-L) jar

3 qt (3 L) natural spring or still mineral water

8 teaspoons (1½ oz/40 g) fine sea salt

1 teaspoon allspice berries

10 black peppercorns

1 fresh bay leaf, crushed

4½ lb (2 kg) green or other firm tomatoes

2 long red chiles, sliced

5 garlic cloves, sliced

4 celery ribs with leaves, leaves separated and stalks chopped

You will also need a 5½-qt (5.5-L) sterilized preserving jar, cheesecloth pressed with a hot iron to sterilize it, and a ceramic or glass dish or jar that will fit inside the neck of the preserving jar

Put the water into a large pan, add the salt, and heat gently, stirring, until dissolved. Add the allspice berries, peppercorns, and bay and bring to a boil, then leave to cool completely.

Meanwhile, make 2 slashes in the form of a cross in the base of each tomato. Stuff each tomato where you have slashed it with 1–2 slices of chile and garlic and some celery leaves.

Put some of the chopped celery ribs into the base of the sterilized preserving jar, then pack the stuffed tomatoes on top. Add some more celery to the very top of the jar (place some long stalks across the top to keep the tomatoes submerged) and pour the brine over. Cover the top of the jar with a piece of the cheesecloth, then insert a small dish or jar partially filled with water into the top of the jar to weight down the ingredients and keep them submerged.

Leave the jar in the kitchen to ferment for 4–10 days, depending on how warm the environment is – the warmer, the quicker they will ferment. Clean and change the cheesecloth every day. If you see mold appearing, do not panic – just remove it carefully with a spoon. You are looking for the water to start bubbling and for the tomatoes to soften and go slightly fizzy. Once they are pleasantly fizzy and sour, store the jar in the refrigerator or in a cellar or other cold place to slow down the fermentation process. They should keep for up to 2 months. If the brine turns slimy, unfortunately it's game over.

Fermented beet & cauliflower

This is another recipe from my Armenian relatives, although of course used to color and flavor pickles all over the Caucasus and the Middle East. There is something very special about coupling it with cauliflower. The textures, the color, the flavor; everything sings. I urge you to make this one – winter will never have felt this vibrant. And do experiment with flavorings, such as adding a few sprigs of hard herbs, such as thyme, or pink peppercorns. This is not the traditional approach, but flavors like ginger, orange, and cumin and coriander seeds would also be welcome additions here.

Makes a 3-qt (3-L) jar
1 qt (1 L) natural spring or still mineral water

5 teaspoons (1 oz/25 g) fine sea salt

10 allspice berries

2 bay leaves

4 beets

1 cauliflower (I use Romanesco)

15 garlic cloves, separated and unpeeled

stick of celery

You will also need a sterilized 3-qt (3-L) preserving jar and cheesecloth pressed with a hot iron to sterilize it

Put the water into a large pan, add the salt, and heat gently, stirring, until dissolved. Add the allspice and bay (or whatever aromatics you choose) and bring to a boil, then leave to cool completely.

Peel the beets and slice into thin wedges. Separate the cauliflower into florets, slicing in half if large, and chop the stalk. Pack the vegetables into your sterilized jar.

Pour the cooled brine and aromatics over the beet and cauliflower. Make sure the vegetables are fully submerged in the brine – I wedge a stick of celery across the neck of the jar to hold everything else down.

Cover the jar with a piece of the cheesecloth and leave in your kitchen for about 5 days, cleaning and changing the cheesecloth every day. The timing really depends on how warm your kitchen is, but you are looking for bubbles and for the vegetables to soften slightly but still be firm and pleasantly sour. Once ready, remove the celery and cheesecloth, seal the jar, and keep in a cool, dark place for up to 2 months.

Tips If you should make your own homemade kefir, sprinkle a couple of drops into the brine in the preserving jar, as it will help the good bacteria grow. Watch out for infections, as beet is quite prone to it. But it's not a problem if the celery becomes a little moldy by the end of the process – just chuck it away.

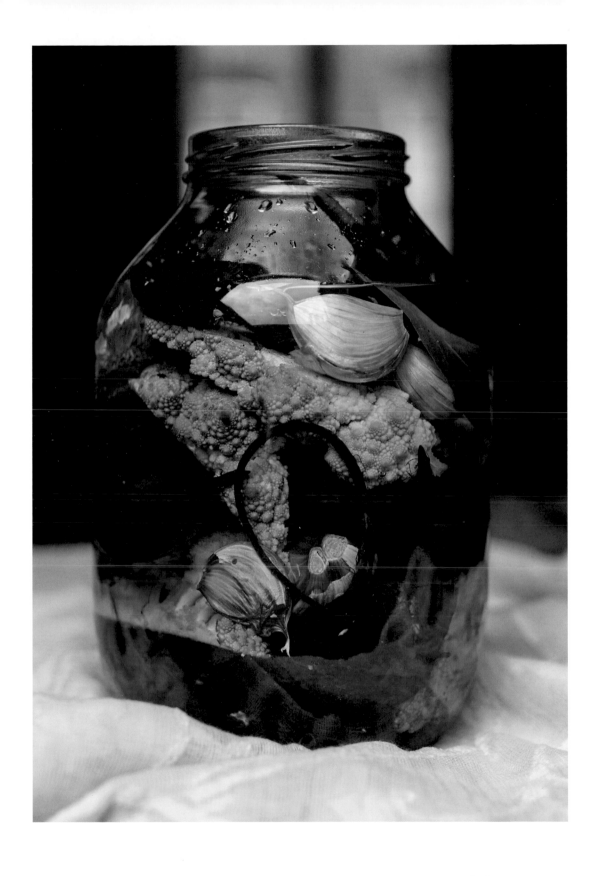

Pickled cherries and the gang

We mostly ferment in Ukraine and Georgia, so I'm a little funny about vinegar pickles, as I often find them too strong, but in Azerbaijan they do use vinegar for pickling and do fantastic things with the pickles. Pickled cherries were a huge revelation to me – they are simply to die for. They are also extremely easy to make, and this way of pickling can be used for many fruits and vegetables. Try this with cauliflower florets, grapes, cucumbers, or, less traditionally, daikon, thinly sliced crab apples, or fennel. These are great served with some buttery *plov* (see pages 120 and 128) and a rich lamb or duck dish, or Lyulya Kebabs (page 152).

Makes a 1-qt (1-L) jar

   1¼ cups (10 fl oz/300 ml) cider vinegar

   4 teaspoons granulated sugar

   2 teaspoons fine sea salt

   5 garlic cloves, peeled and halved

   1 lb (500 g) yellow, red, cornelian, or sour cherries, or grapes

   You will also need a sterilized 1-qt (1-L) preserving jar

Put the vinegar, 6 tablespoons (3 fl oz/100 ml) water, the sugar, and salt in a nonreactive pan and bring to a boil slowly, stirring all the time, so that the sugar dissolves before the water boils.

Turn off the heat, leave to cool, and add the garlic.

Pour the pickling liquid over your cherries, or other fruit or vegetables, packed into your sterilized preserving jar, seal, and leave to pickle in the refrigerator for at least a couple of hours. They can be kept in the pickling liquid in the refrigerator for up to a month.

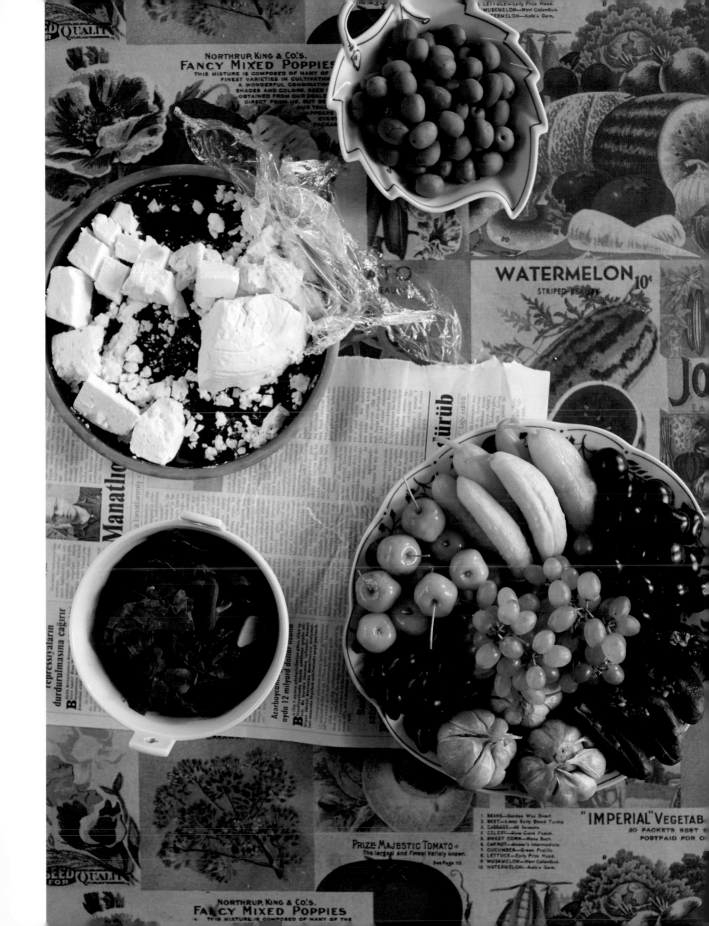

Caucasus is not the place to find a great variety of desserts. Of course, Soviet-era cakes are still made and adapted all over, but as a rule, especially in Azerbaijan, fruit, nuts, and sweet preserves served with a hot strong tea are the norm. There are many types of *pakhlava*, including the most beautiful lace *pakhlava* from Shekhi (west of Azerbaijan) made with rice flour; there are *khalvas* and Georgian and Armenian *churchkhela* (nuts covered in grape must), but there isn't much else. And I don't mind that. Often, after a big feast, I do not feel like eating heavy cake. But do not skip this chapter – I have collected plenty of recipes for those who are sweet in the tooth.

sweet in the tooth

Pakhlava

Pakhlava is a festive dish made for *Novruz*, the traditional celebration of the coming of spring in Azerbaijan, but it's rarely prepared at home, since nuts are expensive and making thin pastry is rather laborious. However, it is a gorgeous thing, and if you like baking and making something new, this is a great way to spend an afternoon, especially if you are cooking with your loved ones. The recipe makes enough to last you a couple of weeks and to package up into gift boxes for friends and family.

Makes about 55 pieces

DOUGH

2 eggs

¾ cup (7 oz/200 g) unsalted butter, melted

⅞ cup (7 oz/200 g) sour cream

2 teaspoons superfine sugar

1 teaspoon (3 g) instant yeast

pinch of salt

6⅔ cups (1¾ lb/800 g) all-purpose flour, plus extra for dusting

SYRUP

2½ cups (17½ oz/500 g) superfine sugar

a pinch of saffron threads

FILLING

1¾ lb (800 g) nuts (walnuts, almonds, and pistachios are all equally good), ground, plus about 55 pieces of nut to decorate

3 cups (1⅓ lb/600 g) superfine sugar

2 tablespoons cardamom pods, toasted and seeds ground

about 2 cups (1 lb/450 g) Clarified Butter (page 53), for brushing

2 eggs, beaten, for glazing

You will also need a baking sheet measuring 10 x 16 inches (25 x 40 cm)

To make the dough, mix the eggs with the melted butter, sour cream, 2 teaspoons sugar, and yeast in a large bowl. Mix the salt into the flour, then gradually add the flour to the liquid ingredients, first mixing with a wooden spoon and then working the mixture with your hands into a firm dough. Cover with a damp kitchen towel and leave to rest for 30 minutes.

For the syrup, put ¾ cup (6 fl oz/175 ml) water, the 2½ cups sugar, and the saffron into a pan and bring to a boil slowly, stirring all the time, so that the sugar dissolves before the water starts boiling. Leave to cool.

Mix all the filling ingredients together in a bowl and set aside.

Divide the dough into 8 balls – 2 of them (for the top and bottom layer) should be 12 oz (350 g) each, the other 6 should be 3½ oz (100 g) each.

Line the baking sheet with baking parchment, with enough excess all round so that you can use it to manipulate and lift the *pakhlava* out, and brush the paper with clarified butter.

Flour your work surface and press one of the 12-oz (350-g) pieces of dough down with your hand into a disc. Then using a (preferably) thin rolling pin, roll the dough into a 10 x 16–inch (25 x 40–cm) rectangle and place it on the lined sheet. Brush with clarified butter and sprinkle with some of the filling.

Roll out each 3½-oz (100-g) piece of dough, one by one, as thinly as you can into the same size rectangle as before and then layer into the sheet, again brushing each sheet of dough with the clarified butter and adding a sprinkling of the filling.

Roll out the remaining 12-oz (350-g) piece of dough to fit the sheet and pop it on top of the other layers. Press the *pakhlava* gently with the palm of your hand. Now grab the ends of the baking parchment and swiftly fold them over the dough and bring them back again in order to tidy up the shape of the *pakhlava*. Do the same with each side, and then twist each corner of the parchment to make it easier to lift the whole thing out once baked.

Cut the *pakhlava* lengthwise into 7 vertical strips, and then into 12 on the diagonal to create about 55 diamonds – enough to last you a couple of weeks and make gift boxes for friends.

Preheat the oven to 400°F (200°C). Brush the top of the *pakhlava* with the egg glaze and press a piece of nut into the middle of each diamond. Bake for 15–20 minutes, then remove from the oven and drizzle over the rest of the clarified butter. Reduce the oven temperature to 350°F (180°C) and return the *pakhlava* to the oven until the top layer is golden and crispy, 25 minutes more.

Take the *pakhlava* out of the oven and drizzle with the saffron syrup, then go over the cuts again with a knife and drizzle the syrup between the layers, too. Leave the *pakhlava* to settle for a bit, then lift it out carefully (like lifting a body on a stretcher) using the twisted baking parchment corners and with somebody's help. Run along the cuts again and then store the pieces in an airtight container, out of the refrigerator, for up to a week, or in the refrigerator for up to a month; if the latter, make sure you take it out 2 hours before serving so that the clarified butter isn't too hard.

Nana's pinecone muffins

Marina Nariashvili runs her own guesthouse in Akhaltsikhe in southern Georgia, and she creates all sorts of incredible things from pinecones. Her daughter-in-law Nana also makes excellent food and possesses one of the most serene, beautiful faces I have ever encountered – gentle but strong, as if out of a painting. This is one of Nana's recipes, although I must admit that the original had twice as much sugar. I prefer them less sweet, especially if they are dipped in the cocoa dulce de leche sauce. But if you aren't serving them with the sauce, please do add more sugar.

Makes 12 muffins
- ¾ cup (5 oz/150 g) superfine sugar
- 1 egg
- ¾ cup (6 oz/175 g) Homemade Matsoni (page 29) or plain yogurt
- 2 tablespoons sunflower oil
- 1⅔ cup (7 oz/200 g) all-purpose flour
- 1 teaspoon baking soda
- ½ teaspoon baking powder

- 12 small young green pinecones (optional)
- Clementine Preserve juice (see page 210), to glaze

DIPPING SAUCE
- ¾ cup (7 oz/200 g) unsalted butter
- ¾ cup (9 oz/250 g) dulce de leche or Anna's Sweet Milk (page 220)
- 3 tablespoons superfine sugar
- 5 tablespoons cocoa powder

Preheat the oven to 350°F (180°C). Lightly oil a 12-cup muffin pan or line with paper liners.

Beat the sugar and egg together in a bowl until light and fluffy, then fold in the *matsoni* and the oil.

In a separate bowl, sift the flour with the baking soda and baking powder, then fold into the liquid ingredients.

Fill the muffin cups a little more than two-thirds full with the muffin mixture, then bake in the oven until well risen and golden brown, about 30 minutes. Five minutes before the end of the baking time, add a pinecone to the top of each muffin, if using, and brush with some clementine preserve juice to glaze. Remove the muffins from the oven and leave to cool slightly on a wire rack.

For the dipping sauce, mix all the ingredients together in a saucepan, set over low heat, and stir just until the mixture has completely melted – don't cook it for any longer. Dip the tops of the muffins into the sauce and serve straight away.

Pine flower honey

It's springtime again, and Marina heads out to collect pine flower buds. They are covered in a little "skirt," which is removed and then the flower buds pounded, their golden dust (pollen) showering everywhere. Marina gives pinecone flower honey to her grandchildren every morning, as it's believed to be beneficial for the lungs. Try this honey on pancakes!

Makes a 1-qt (1-L) jar
  1 lb (500 g) pine flower buds
  4 cups (1⅔ lb/750 g) wild flower honey

  You will also need a clean 1-qt (1-L) airtight jar

Mince the flowers in a meat grinder, if you have one, or bash them using a mortar and pestle.

Mix the minced or pounded flowers through the honey until well incorporated.

Pour the honey into the jar, seal, and store in a cool, dry place.

Pinecone conserve

Marina Nariashvili's guesthouse in southern Georgia is surrounded by pine forests. Her many grandchildren all have little blankets for taking a nap under the pine trees during the day or to meditate, in the lotus position in the case of her eight-year-old granddaughter! Come May, Marina ventures deeper into the forest to forage for little young pinecones to turn into all sorts of wonderful things, including this conserve. Serve it with drop scones or with the Pinecone Muffins (page 195).

Makes a 3½-qt (3.5-L) jar
  1 qt (1 L) water
  7½ cups (3¼ lb/1.5 kg) granulated sugar
  2¼ lb (1 kg) young green pinecones
  1 teaspoon citric acid

  You will also need a sugar thermometer

Put the water into a large pan, add the sugar, and heat gently, stirring, until dissolved.

Add the pinecones and continue cooking the syrup until it reaches a temperature of 234–240°F (112–116°C) on the thermometer, or soft-ball stage, which will take about 30 minutes.

Add the citric acid, then leave the mixture to cool before using. If the syrup is too liquid once cooled, reheat and cook for a few minutes more. It will store unopened for a few months.

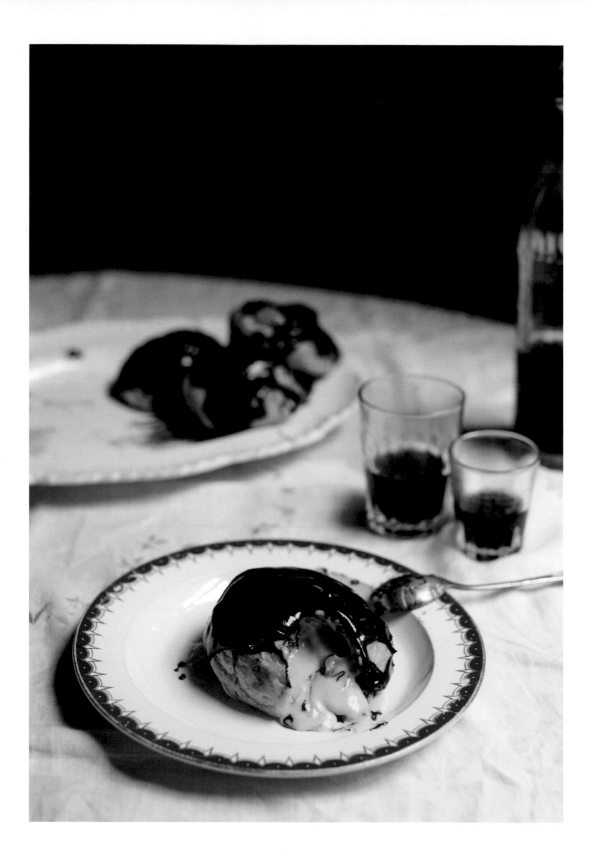

Armenian "cognac" profiteroles

There was something about Soviet-era Armenian "cognac." It was actually just a brandy and I'm not sure how good it really was, probably not very. I normally hate desserts with alcohol, which must be down to the bad-quality chocolates filled with sickly sour cherry liqueur that we were all too familiar with growing up, but there was and still is one exception – my mum's profiteroles that she would lace with lashings of this cognac when we were little. My mum doesn't even remember that she used to make them and in fact now denies she ever did! But I will never forget that lovely hit of alcohol in luscious crème mousseline made with raw milk and thickened with butter. The choux pastry recipe is based on the one that I was taught at Leiths School of Food and Wine, and it is foolproof. If you can't find Armenian brandy, use a little dash of Armagnac. Or try a splash of Tia Maria – almost as classy as the Armenian stuff! Sarcasm aside, it does deliver an amazing, subtle flavor and is also very good used in a tiramisu.

Makes about 12 large profiteroles

CHOUX PASTRY
  6 tablespoons (3 oz/85 g) unsalted butter, cut into cubes
  ⅞ cup (3¾ oz/105 g) all-purpose flour
  pinch of salt
  3 eggs, at room temperature, lightly beaten

CRÈME MOUSSELINE
  2 cups (16 fl oz/450 ml) milk
  1 vanilla pod, split lengthwise and seeds scraped out, pod reserved
  5 egg yolks
  ½ cup (3½ oz/100 g) superfine sugar
  ⅔ cup (2¾ oz/75 g) all-purpose flour
  ¼ cup (2 fl oz/50 ml) Armenian brandy or equivalent (your favorite)
  3 tablespoons (1¾ oz/50 g) unsalted butter, cut into pieces

Preheat the oven to 400°F (200°C). Line 2 large baking sheets with baking parchment.

To make the choux pastry, put 1 cup (8 fl oz/220 ml) water and the butter into a saucepan and warm it over low heat so that the butter melts but the water doesn't boil and evaporate.

Sift the flour over a sheet of baking parchment, then fold and seal one end of the paper to create a pocket. You basically have to dump all the flour in one go into the hot water (we called it "bombing it"), and this makes it easier. So with your flour pocket and a wooden spoon at the ready, raise the heat under the pan and wait for the water to boil and rise, and the butter to

continued »

be collected in the center. Shoot the flour in, switch off the heat, and beat the mixture with a wooden spoon until it starts separating from the walls of the pan, turning into a ball.

Spread the mixture over a large plate to help it cool down. Then pop it into a bowl and start beating in the eggs, 1 tablespoon at a time. You are looking for a shiny dough with a reluctant dropping consistency. When one-third of the egg has gone in, lift a bit of dough up on the edge of the wooden spoon and let it drop – it should take 6 seconds for it to drop if the consistency is right.

Spoon large tablespoonfuls of the choux mixture onto the lined baking sheets, allowing some space in between, as the pastry will expand during baking.

Bake until the choux buns are golden and cooked through, 25–30 minutes. Remove from the oven and leave them to cool on a wire rack.

Meanwhile, to make the alcoholic crème mousseline, heat the milk with the vanilla seeds and scraped-out pod in a large saucepan.

Mix the egg yolks with the sugar and the flour in a separate bowl.

When the milk is near boiling point, quickly tip some of it into the egg mixture, stirring vigorously so that the eggs don't scramble. Then tip the egg mixture into the rest of the milk in the pan and cook over medium-low heat, stirring constantly, until the cream thickens to a custard-like consistency, 10–15 minutes.

Add the alcohol and turn off the heat, then add the butter, a piece at a time, whisking to help it melt. Cover the surface with plastic wrap to stop a skin from forming, then leave it to cool completely.

When everything is cooled and you are ready to serve, make a hole at the bottom of each choux bun and use a pastry bag to fill with the crème mousseline.

VARIATION
You can drizzle melted chocolate ganache over the profiteroles, or try dipping them in the cocoa and dulce de leche dipping sauce as with the Pinecone Muffins (page 195).

I have tried filling these with the custard for the Buckwheat Ice Cream (see pages 202–3) with some flour and butter added as per the recipe above, and it was interesting and delicious. And instead of chocolate, I brushed the profiteroles with a little sugar syrup and sprinkled over some toasted buckwheat groats.

Preserved whole peaches

In the Ukraine, we would preserve our summer glut, producing the best "canned" (or rather bottled) fruit known to humanity. Forget the stuff you buy in cans – this is the real deal. Look for the best end-of-summer produce available, and then enjoy the resulting preserved fruits and their fragrant syrup just as they come, biting into the flesh with the juice dribbling down your chin, or in cakes. Dan Lepard, a baker and food writer, devised an amazing cake recipe using canned peaches and almonds that I have been using for years. So here is how you can make this sensuous, callypigian preserve.

Makes a 3-qt (3-L) jar

2½ cups (1 lb/500 g) golden superfine sugar

7 ripe but firm peaches, left whole

You will also need a sterilized 3-qt (3-L) preserving jar

Put 2 qt (2 L) water into a large pan, add the sugar, and heat gently, stirring, until dissolved, then bring to a boil.

Pop the peaches into your sterilized jar – the fruits will hopefully be small enough to be pushed through the neck of the jar. Pour the hot syrup over and leave to cool. When cool, pour the syrup out of the jar into a saucepan (leaving the peaches in the jar) and reheat the syrup again to boiling point, then pour it back over the peaches one more time. Once the syrup cools, the peaches are ready to eat.

The peaches will keep for 1 week in the refrigerator, or, sealed hermetically, for several months in the pantry.

Buckwheat ice cream

I really, really wanted to use Marina's pinecones in a dessert of my own (see pages 195–6), as they are just so unusual, a chef's dream. But because they are so tannic and taste so strongly of pine, only a tiny bit could be used. I also really wanted to make buckwheat ice cream, as when we were children, mum used to boil buckwheat in salted water and then dress it with melted butter and sugar. That flavor was haunting me, just like I imagine the cereal milk would for those who grew up eating sweet cereal. My friend Alissa and I threw a Kino Vino supper club during Russian filmmaker Andrei Tarkovsky Week in London, showing his 1975 film called *Mirror*, followed by a feast inspired by the movie. One of the last scenes depicted a buckwheat field bordering a malachite-hued pine forest. Bingo. The two came together. So this is my poetic nostalgic dessert – although don't worry about trying to find pinecones, as I've suggested using fresh bay leaves instead here to add savoriness.

Serves 6–8

⅔ cup (3½ oz/100 g) raw buckwheat groats (or use pre-toasted)

10 fresh bay leaves, crushed

1 cup (8 fl oz/250 ml) milk

1 cup (8 oz/250 g) heavy cream

generous pinch of salt

4 egg yolks

½–¾ cup (3½–5½ oz/100–150 g) granulated sugar

You will also need (ideally) an ice-cream machine and a large piece of cheesecloth

If using raw buckwheat, heat a large, dry frying pan over medium heat, toss in the buckwheat, and toast, wiggling the pan about from time to time, until it becomes golden but not burnt. Taste it and check that it is crunchy and edible – it's very important that you get this right. Leave the buckwheat to cool.

Wrap the crushed bay leaves and buckwheat in the cheesecloth and tie securely. Add it to the milk and cream in a large saucepan over medium heat. Add the salt and taste the mixture – you should be able to detect the salt ever so slightly.

When the milk mixture is almost boiling, turn the heat off and leave to infuse for an hour.

Beat the egg yolks and granulated sugar together in a large heatproof bowl.

Remove the cheesecloth and squeeze out all the flavor, then discard. Bring the milk mixture back up to almost boiling. Pour it onto the egg yolk mixture, stirring constantly, then pour this mixture back into the pan and cook over low heat, stirring, until slightly thickened, about 5 minutes.

Cover the surface of the custard with plastic wrap to prevent a skin from forming and leave the custard to cool.

Churn the ice cream in an ice-cream machine according to the manufacturer's instructions, then serve with, for example, some simple poached rhubarb.

Tip *If you don't have an ice-cream machine, create a semifreddo with the custard. Make the custard as instructed above and leave to cool, then fold through 4 egg whites, whisked until firm peaks form. Freeze for 2 hours and serve slightly soft.*

Qata

Versions of this cookie recipe exist all over the Caucasus. I was taught this one by my Aunt Nina on the Armenian side of the family. She makes them plain, but I do love nuts in my cookies, so I add either whole or crushed nuts to the buttery filling. My mum also sprinkles sesame seeds over them because, well, any cookie or bread is improved by the addition of sesame, in our opinion.

Makes 30–35 cookies

PASTRY

3⅓ cups (14 oz/400 g) all-purpose flour, plus extra for dusting

2 teaspoons (¼ oz/10 g) baking powder

pinch of salt

1 egg, lightly beaten

⅔ cup (5½ oz/150 g) sour cream

1 teaspoon vanilla extract

1 cup (9 oz/250 g) butter, frozen and coarsely grated

FILLING

¾ cup (7 oz/200 g) unsalted butter, frozen and coarsely grated

1 cup (7 oz/200 g) superfine sugar

1 vanilla pod, split lengthwise and seeds scraped out

1¼ cups (5½ oz/150 g) all-purpose flour

½ cup (1¾ oz/50 g) pecan nuts, toasted and crushed

GLAZE

1 egg yolk, lightly beaten

2 tablespoons sesame seeds

To make the pastry, mix the flour, baking powder, and salt together in a bowl.

Mix the egg, sour cream, and vanilla extract together.

Add the butter to the flour mixture and rub in with your fingertips until the mixture looks like crumbs. Mix in the egg and sour cream mixture and quickly knead into a dough, then cover with plastic wrap and refrigerate for an hour or so.

To make the filling, mix the grated butter, sugar, and vanilla seeds together. Put the flour in a bowl, add the butter mixture, and rub in as you did for the pastry.

Preheat the oven to 350°F (180°C). Dust 2 baking sheets with flour.

Divide the pastry in half. Working quickly, flatten each half with your hand and then roll out on a floured work surface into a sheet ¼ inch (5 mm) thick.

Mix the pecan nuts into the filling and spread it over each pastry sheet (or dot it around evenly if your dough is too soft and delicate), leaving a narrow border around the edges.

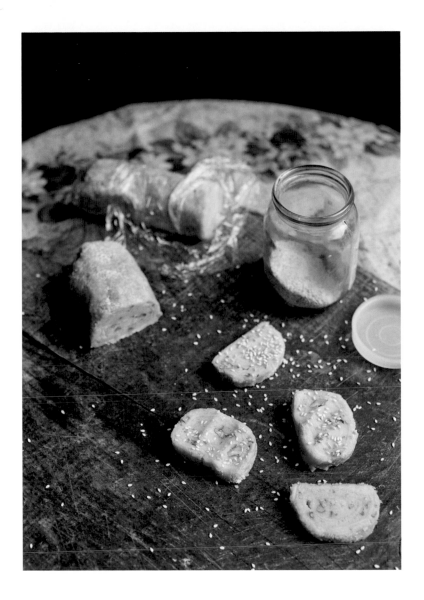

Roll each pastry sheet up into a long sausage as firmly as you can, manipulating the sausage so it is the same thickness all the way along. Put it into the refrigerator for 15 minutes to firm up.

Position the sausages seam side down on your work surface, then brush with the beaten egg yolk and sprinkle with the sesame seeds. Dip a knife in hot water and slice each sausage into discs ¾ inch (2 cm) thick. Place the discs flat on the prepared baking sheets 3 inches (8 cm) apart and squash them slightly with your hands. Put back into the refrigerator for 30 minutes – if they are firm before baking they will hold their shape better. Bake until golden brown, 25–30 minutes. Leave to cool a little on a wire rack, and serve warm.

Three-ears with khalva khasan

It has been really quite difficult to find dessert recipes for this book. Caucasus people simply don't have a prominent baking culture. Sweet strong tea or fruit (fresh or dried), jams, and nuts are what you have at the end of a meal. So whenever I met anyone on my travels in the region, I would really try to tickle their memory to see if they recalled anything special from their childhood. When I visited a family in the hills of Qebele with their endless chestnut trees, it turned out that they made sweet samosas with filo pastry filled with walnut and sugar paste. But then Halima, the eighty-year-old babushka, remembered what she called *khalva khasan* as her favorite, rare childhood treat. She described it as a paste made using chestnuts, hazelnuts, and sugar. The three-eared samosa provides the perfect shell for this *khalva khasan*.

Makes 24

¾ cup (4¼ oz/120 g) cooked and peeled chestnuts (or vacuum-packed)

6 tablespoons (2¼ oz/60 g) hazelnuts, toasted

generous ½ cup (2¼ oz/60 g) walnuts, toasted

⅓ cup (2¼ oz/60 g) granulated sugar

1 vanilla pod, split lengthwise and seeds scraped out

8 oz (240 g) filo pastry sheets (about 6 sheets)

7 tablespoons (3½ oz/100 g) unsalted butter, melted

2 egg yolks mixed with 1 tablespoon milk, to glaze

Preheat the oven to 350°F (180°C).

First, pound all the nuts, sugar, and vanilla seeds together using a mortar and pestle, or blitz to a paste in a powerful blender or food processor. Your filling is ready.

Keeping the filo sheets covered by a damp kitchen towel so that they don't dry out, take one sheet and lay it on the work surface in front of you with the shorter edge nearest you. Brush it lightly with melted butter, then slice it vertically into 4 long strips.

Place a tablespoonful of the filling at the bottom of each strip and fold the bottom right-hand corner up, over the filling. Then do the same with the bottom left-hand corner. Continue folding the strip in triangles until you reach the top and you have a beautiful little samosa. Repeat with the rest of the filo and filling to make 24 dainty pastries.

Place the pastries on a large baking sheet, brush with the egg yolk mixture to glaze, and bake until golden and crisp, 8 minutes. Serve with some strong black tea. Store any leftovers in an airtight container – they should keep for up to 1 week.

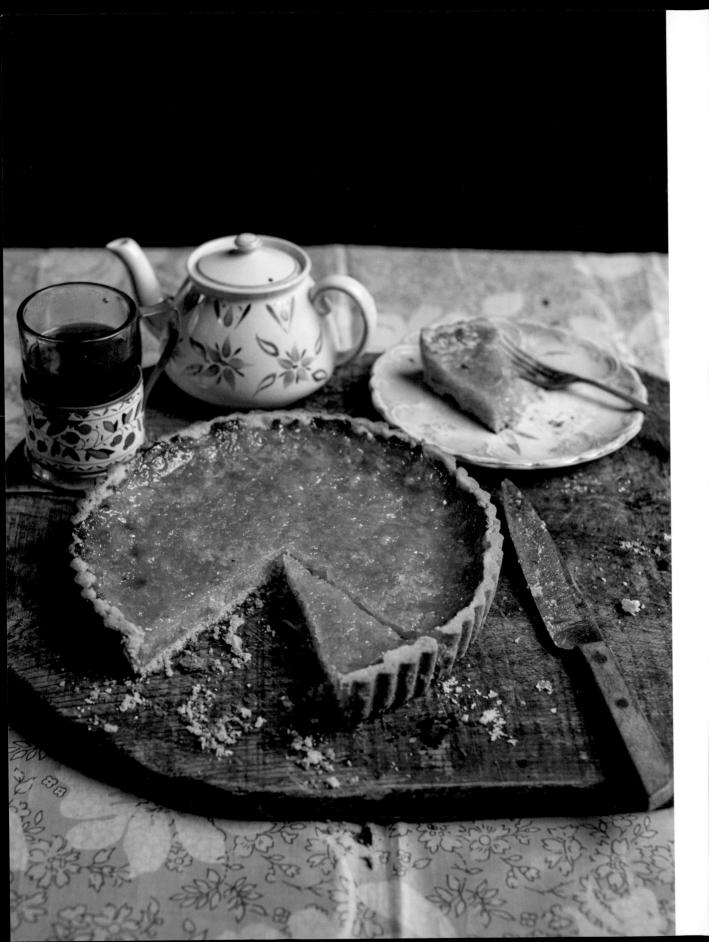

Valya's lemon tart

Azerbaijani cuisine is not renowned for its desserts, so Zulfiya was fortunate in having Valentina, a Russian woman, as a family friend who makes sweet creations. She may have had an influence on Zulya, who besides being a concert pianist and piano teacher at a conservatory in Baku is now also a pastry shop owner, as she gives her desserts musical names, thereby bringing both her worlds together. I am giving the original recipe here, which features the use of vinegar, an acid, as a catalyst for the baking soda to act as a rising agent. This technique was widely used in the Soviet Union because yeast was often scarce.

Serves 6–8

FILLING
- 3–4 large lemons
- boiling water, as needed
- 1¼ cups (9 oz/250 g) superfine sugar
- 2 egg yolks, beaten, for glazing

PASTRY
- 1⅞ cups (8 oz/225 g) all-purpose flour
- generous pinch of salt
- 7 tablespoons (3¼ oz/100 g) cold unsalted butter, diced
- 1 teaspoon cider vinegar
- ½ teaspoon baking soda

To start the filling, cover the lemons with boiling water and leave for 20 minutes, then drain and leave to cool. Place them in the freezer until frozen, at least 2 hours.

For the pastry, sift the flour and salt together into a large bowl, then rub in the cold butter until the mixture resembles fine bread crumbs. Alternatively, chill the flour in a container in the refrigerator and then add the salt and blitz it with the cold butter in a food processor.

Add the vinegar to the baking soda, which will make it foam, then add a splash of water. Mix the liquid into the flour and butter mixture to bind it into a dough. Wrap the dough in plastic wrap and chill in the refrigerator for at least an hour.

Preheat the oven to 350°F (180°C).

Roll out the pastry and use to line a 9½-inch (24-cm) tart pan. Line the pastry shell with baking parchment, fill with ceramic pie weights, and bake blind for 5 minutes, then remove the weights and paper and bake for another 5 minutes.

Remove the lemons from the freezer and grate them coarsely (this will be hard and cold, but hang in there!). Mix the grated lemons with the sugar, then use to fill the pastry shell. Use a pastry brush to dab with the egg glaze. Bake until the filling has set to a marmalade-like consistency, 35–40 minutes. Leave to cool before serving. This is a strong-tasting dessert, so have a small piece with a cup of strong tea without milk.

Clementine preserve

Clementines and mandarins were in huge deficit when I was growing up, a special treat reserved for Christmas. I clearly remember burying myself in yet another book under a scratchy blanket sucking the juice out of every segment of a clementine, then chewing on the empty membrane, one by one until all the mandarins I nicked from the kitchen were gone and I had to procure another tasty snack. Reading and eating were the biggest pleasures in my life at that point. Those precious clementines were from the southwestern Georgian region of Adjara, a mountainous tropical beauty of a land, with rows and rows of clementine and persimmon trees. They make a pretty simple clementine preserve there, still juicy and not too sweet, and here's my version – a new favorite way to eat this fruit.

Makes 1½ lb (650 g)

   1 lb (500 g) clementines

   1½ cups (10½ oz/300 g) superfine sugar

   1 cinnamon stick

   juice of ½ lemon

   You will also need three 8-oz (225-g) sterilized airtight jars

Cover the whole, unpeeled clementines with cold water in a bowl and leave to soak overnight.

The next morning, cut the clementines in half along the equator and then into half moons ¼ inch (5 mm) thick.

Add the sugar and 1¼ cups (10 fl oz/300 ml) water to the fruit and again leave overnight.

Transfer the entire contents of the bowl to a medium saucepan along with the cinnamon stick and cook over low heat for 1¼ hours.

Add the lemon juice and cook for another 15 minutes, or until set to your liking.

Pour the hot preserve into the warm sterilized jars, seal, and leave to cool, then store in a cool, dark place. It should keep unopened for up to a year.

Tip Marina from Akhaltsikhe rolls the citrus peel into pretty little curls before jarring – an example of intense marmalade dedication that I've never seen before.

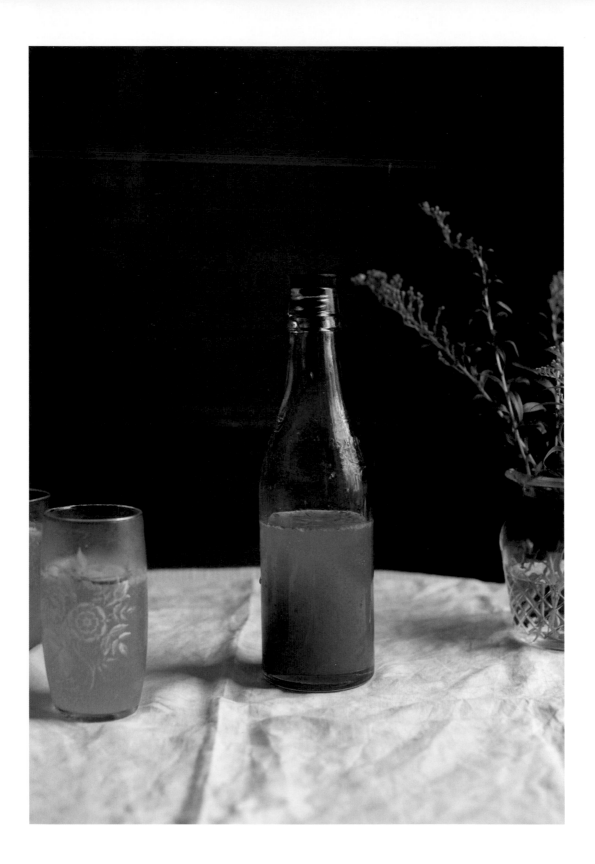

Tarragon & cucumber lemonade

Instead of cola and fizzy orange drinks, us ex-Soviet children grew up drinking a fizzy fluorescent green pop called *tarkhun*, meaning "tarragon." It was poisonous-green, very sweet, yet somehow delicious. Tarragon is extremely popular in Georgia – they do not shy away from its strong flavor. I do love adding cucumbers, like they do in the Pheasant's Tears restaurant in Signagi, a town in the Kakheti region of eastern Georgia, which makes this summer drink even fresher.

Makes about 3 qt (3 L)
    1 cup (7 oz/200 g) superfine sugar
    finely grated zest and juice of 4 lemons
    2 bunches of tarragon
    2 cucumbers, sliced
    2 qt (2 L) cold sparkling mineral water

Put 2 cups (16 fl oz/500 ml) water in a saucepan with the sugar and heat over low heat, stirring often, until the sugar has completely dissolved. Leave to cool completely, then stir in the lemon zest and juice.

Blitz the tarragon (reserving a few sprigs) and half the cucumber in a blender or food processor (easier and less splashy than using a mortar and pestle, although you can do it that way). Strain the mixture through a fine sieve.

Mix the lemony cordial with the tarragon and cucumber juice and dilute it as you would any cordial – top up with sparkling or still water. Garnish with the reserved tarragon sprigs and the remaining cucumber slices. This is not too bad with a dash of gin, too.

Tklapi or plum fruit leather

Fruit leathers are a big thing in the Caucasus. It is simply another way to preserve a glut of fruit and every kind is used, from small tart plums to mulberries, cherries, apricots, and even kiwifruit. They make a beautiful healthy snack, but also add a subtle sweet and sour note to stews and soups. In Akhaltsikhe, a small city in southern Georgia, I visited Galina's house and found her holding a giant oar of a wooden spoon that she was using to stir about 5 gallons of plum pulp in a huge cauldron on top of a wood fire. It was mid-afternoon and still hot even though it was the end of September. Galina was reducing the liquid until it thickened and was almost syrupy. Her daughters-in-law and little grandson were there to help and cover the long outside table with white linen sheets. They poured the hot purée on top of the linen sheets and spread it into a thin layer. It was left to set and dry in the sun, hanging over a washing line. When dry, it is unpeeled and folded, and kept over winter in a dark, dry place.

Makes two 12 x 16-inch (30 x 40-cm) sheets
  2¼ lb (1 kg) ripe plums (or apricots, apples, mulberries, strawberries, or cherries)
  ¼ cup (1¾ oz/50 g) superfine sugar or honey (adjust depending on sweetness of fruit)
  juice of 1 lemon

Put your plums into a large stockpot or preserving pan and add a splash of water. Heat over medium heat until the mixture starts bubbling, then reduce the heat and cook until the plums have collapsed, about 30 minutes. Stir from time to time, and if it looks like there isn't enough moisture, add another splash of water. Strain through a fine-mesh sieve into a large bowl, discarding the pits and skin.

Place the plum flesh back in the cleaned pan, add the sugar or honey and lemon juice, and cook over low heat until the sugar, if using, has dissolved, then simmer for about 40–60 minutes. You are aiming for a smooth and thick purée, about 1¼ lb (600 g) in quantity.

Meanwhile, preheat the oven to 200°F (100°C) and line 2 large baking sheets with nonstick baking parchment.

Ladle some of the hot fruit purée all over the lined sheets, then spread it thinly – the fruit leather should be almost transparent. Leave it to dry in the oven for about 12 hours. The leather should be thoroughly dry and peel away from the parchment easily. Then just fold it into quarters and wrap in baking parchment. It will keep somewhere dark and dry for 6 months.

Tip *This method can be applied to most types of fruit, as the whole point of the recipe is to preserve overripe, surplus fruit in September – it just has to be of good quality and very ripe.*

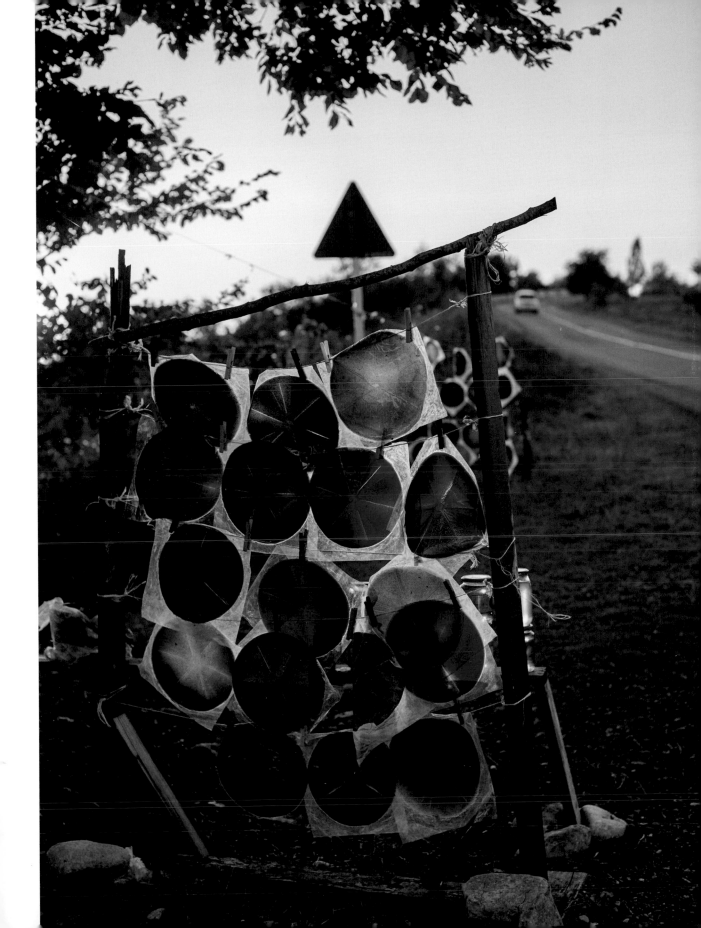

Basil sherbet

They love a sherbet in Azerbaijan. It is basically an infused fruit or spiced sugar syrup diluted with cold water.

Makes 1 qt (1 L)
- 1 qt (1 L) hot water
- 1 bunch of purple or green basil, or Thai basil, leaves and stalks separated
- juice of 4 lemons, plus extra to taste
- ¾ cup (3½ oz/100 g) agave syrup, plus extra to taste
- crushed ice, to serve

Pour the hot (but not boiling) water over the basil stalks in a bowl and leave to stand and infuse until it cools down. The water will turn purple if using purple basil!

Mix the lemon juice with the agave syrup in a separate bowl, then add the basil leaves and muddle them together a little.

Strain the stalks out of the water and then stir the infused water into the lemon and basil leaf mixture. Taste it and add more lemon or agave as you wish. Serve with some crushed ice.

Keti's tea

Irish coffee? Try Georgian tea. In the Kazbegi mountains in northeastern Georgia, Keti gave us some herbal tea. I couldn't put my finger on why this herbal tea was so incredible. I kept drinking it, with my eyes getting wider and wider. "What is this? Is this some kind of crazy wild berry?" I asked Keti. She smiled wryly – it turns out that she had sweetened it with vanilla sugar and spiked it with brandy!

Don't worry if you can't find exactly the same dried wild herbs – any combination of aromatics will work. It is the addition of brandy and vanilla that turns this tea into something quite delicious.

Serves 4–6
- ⅛ oz (5 g) dried wild thyme
- ¼ oz (10 g) rosehips
- ⅛ oz (5 g) dried barberries
- ⅛ oz (5 g) black tea leaves
- handful of dried citrus peel
- ¼ vanilla pod or 1 tablespoon vanilla sugar
- splash of good brandy

Pop everything except the brandy into a teapot and cover with boiling water.

Leave to infuse for about 5 minutes, then add the brandy.

Anna's sweet milk

A lady I met called Zhuzhuna Bardzimadze from Akhaltsikhe had the kindest face and tastiest pickles. She lives, like so many others in Georgia, with her son and Kakhetian daughter-in-law Anna. Anna makes the sweetest milk – a proper homemade dulce de leche, and by that I don't mean boiling store-bought condensed milk! This is the real deal. I loved that she knew that the amount the recipe made would vary depending on the season, due to the difference in the fat content of the milk. In August, for instance, her yield was always bigger, as the milk is fattier. The Georgians make cakes with this or just eat it spread on a bit of bread.

Makes about 3 cups (24 fl oz/700 ml)

½ gallon (64 fl oz/2 L) cow's milk or goat's milk

1¾ cups (12 oz/350 g) superfine sugar

1 vanilla pod, split lengthwise and seeds scraped out

1 teaspoon sea salt flakes

1 teaspoon baking soda

Bring the milk, sugar, vanilla seeds, and salt to a boil in a large saucepan (it needs to be a tall saucepan, as the milk will rise and froth once the baking soda is added).

Take the pan off the heat and add the baking soda. Stir it and it will start to foam and rise rapidly (tap the base of the pan with a wooden spoon to stop it).

When it calms down, put the pan back on the heat and gently simmer over low heat, stirring from time to time to ensure it doesn't burn on the bottom, and taking care not to let it boil, or the milk can curdle. Cook until the milk turns darker in color (it should look like café au lait color at this point), 30–40 minutes. When the mixture thickens and is the consistency of heavy cream, really watch it and start whisking continuously to prevent curdling. As it thickens, keep whisking until it reduces right down. Once the mixture has become viscous and brown like toasted hazelnuts, it's ready.

Tip *If the mixture looks curdled, it can be saved by reheating and whisking in a couple of tablespoons of milk.*

Opposite: Zhuzhuna and her son.

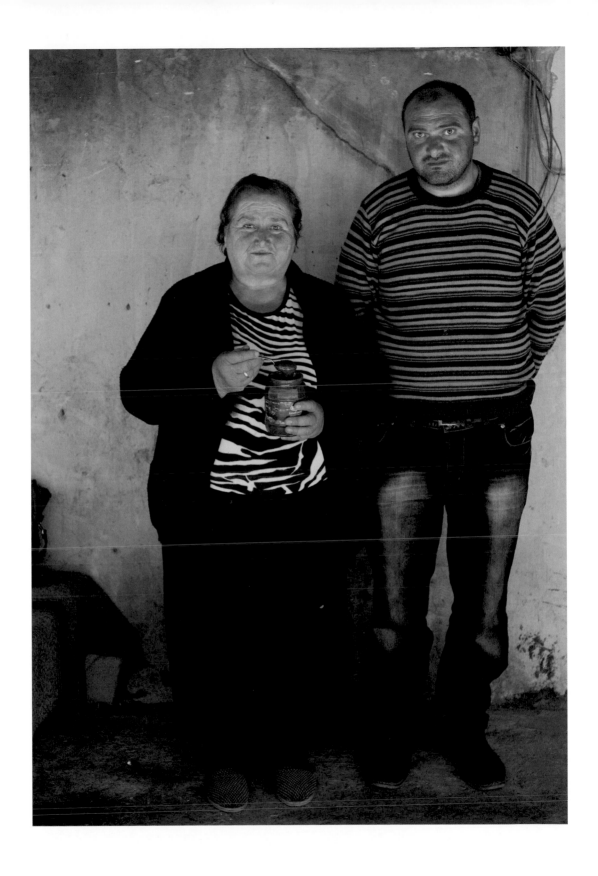

Liliana's lemon & dulce de leche cake

Elena, the book's photographer, is half-Argentinian. When Anna brought along a jar of her homemade condensed milk, Elena's face lit up. "I know my dulce de leche," she remarked with a twinkle in her eye and a wry smile. She tried it and smiled again, declaring, "It's good, it's very good!" And then she told me that her mum, Liliana, made a lemon and dulce de leche cake, which sounded so good. It turned out even better, as there was a suitably sweet story attached to it. It's about Liliana's third child Hanry, who was born between lunch and this cake on October 1, 1989. It goes like this, in her own words: "Contractions started in the morning, so I thought I should bake a cake, as Dr. Michel Odent was coming to assist me. I went shopping so that I had all the ingredients, I made the cake, and my mother prepared lunch. Sunday lunch . . . I was so hungry! But when the lemon and dulce de leche cake was approaching the table, I stood up and shouted: 'No cake, baby is coming!' And I took refuge in a bedroom. Only an hour and a half later, my nine-pound boy was born. At this point I asked his father: 'Could you hold the baby so that I can eat the cake?' And he replied: 'I would love to . . . but the cord is short . . . !' I was still attached to the baby, as the placenta had not yet been delivered!" This story made me happy. The end.

Serves 6–8

grated zest and juice of 1 lemon

¼ oz (10 g) lemon verbena leaves, bruised (optional)

2½ tablespoons confectioners' sugar

¾ cup (7 oz/200 g) unsalted butter, softened, plus extra for greasing

1 cup (7 oz/200 g) superfine sugar

2 eggs, lightly beaten

1⅔ cups (7 oz/200 g) self-rising flour

¾ cup (6 fl oz/200 ml) dulce de leche or Anna's Sweet Milk (page 220)

edible flowers, such as borage or cornflowers, to decorate

To make the drizzle, mix the lemon juice with the bruised verbena leaves, if using, in a bowl and leave to infuse for at least 30 minutes. Then whisk in the confectioners' sugar, making sure that it dissolves.

Preheat the oven to 350°F (180°C). Grease an 8½-inch (22-cm) cake pan and line it with baking parchment.

Using an electric mixer fitted with a paddle attachment, beat the butter and superfine sugar together until really pale and fluffy. Then gradually add the eggs and the lemon zest, beating well after each addition.

Fold the flour through the cake mixture gently, then pour the cake mixture into the prepared pan. Bake until a skewer comes out clean, 30 minutes.

Leave the cake to cool in the pan for a few minutes, then turn out onto a wire rack, remove the lining paper, and leave to cool completely.

Cut the cake in half horizontally and spread the dulce de leche on the bottom layer, then cover with the top layer. Brush the drizzle over the top of the cake (it will soak in), scatter with edible flowers to decorate, and serve.

Ingredients

Caucasian food, at least in the ex–Soviet Union region, has always had a reputation for being meat-heavy. However, while Russian *shashlyki* or Georgian *mtsvadi* or Azerbaijani *shish* kebabs are commonly served in restaurants, in the modest everyday lives of most people in the Caucasus, especially in rural areas, meat is considered a treat – as it should be. Sheep as well as other animals are well reared in small numbers, and the meat is of superb quality. My grandparents in the south of Ukraine managed to rear their own animals despite the stratospheric rise of Soviet industrialization, enjoying meat only on occasion and making use of every part of the slaughtered beast without any waste.

When I had finished writing this book, I surprised myself at the size of the vegetarian chapter – it was the longest. I tried balancing it out with more meat recipes but then decided that, if vegetables, legumes, bread, and dairy are the heroes of everyday eating, I shouldn't force the meat chapter to be bigger. And to be honest, vegetable dishes are the ones that I personally find the most interesting. It's all about the hits of flavor that such simple fresh ingredients can deliver when put to unexpected use. Pound mint, salt, and green chile together, for instance, and use to season mozzarella or lamb chops or stir through new potatoes or roasted vegetables. Or make some *matsoni* (homemade yogurt; see page 29) and serve it with tender runner beans.

People in the Caucasus are still so connected to their local land and its produce, and more often than not these ingredients are beyond excellent – you can taste the love and care that went into growing them. And foraging for them is not a trendy buzzword – harvesting nature's gifts is still a way of life, and what a rewarding way it is.

The following are some ingredients that may throw you, but if you want to experience the authentic flavors of the Caucasus, I strongly recommend sourcing them, and I have listed a number of suppliers to help you (see page 234). A jar of blue fenugreek, some dried marigold petals, and *adjika* salt will last you ages. But if you can't find some of these exotic ingredients, it's not the end of the world; Adjapsandali (page 41), for example, will remain incredible even if it doesn't see any blue fenugreek. This is a food-lovers' book, so all you really need is good-quality produce – great vegetables, small amounts of excellent meat, a few spices, and some raw creamy milk if you would like to have a go at making fresh cheese (see page 107). Don't let the constraints of a written recipe hold you back – buy some fresh vegetables from your farmers' market, be creative with substitutions, and open your mind to new techniques. Cooking should not be a robotic act: instinct, intuition, and constant tasting and adjusting the flavor balance are essential skills that will help you become an outstanding cook, just like the Caucasians. They use traditional recipes, sure, but they are also some of the most creative cooks I have ever come across. How can you fail to be with ingredients so outstanding?

Spices

BLUE FENUGREEK

Utskho-suneli, as Georgians call blue fenugreek so sonorously, or *Trigonella caerulea*, as botanists term it a little more brashly, is said to be endemic to Georgia, even though *utskho-suneli* means "foreign spice." In its dried ground form, it is one of the components of the Georgian *khmeli-suneli* spice mix (see below), so if you can't find it on its own, source the spice mix online and you will get a taste of that funky Georgian flavor into your dishes. Some say that the smell and taste reminds them of the standard fenugreek used in Indian cooking, albeit milder. I agree that it is subtle, but to me it has very little to do with the bitter fenugreek that we are more familiar with in the West, its flavor being more akin to the most complex yet gentle garam masala. When you experience good-quality blue fenugreek, try as you may to register that it's just one spice, it smells like a heady mixture of ten spices.

KHMELI-SUNELI

This is Georgia's famous spice mix, which varies in constitution and can contain up to twenty different dried herbs and spices. It usually features dried blue fenugreek leaves and seeds, coriander, fennel, cloves, marigold, mint, dill seeds, and summer savory, but may also include dill, marjoram, hyssop, parsley, basil, bay, cassia bark, and even a little hot chile. You can use a little of this instead of blue fenugreek on its own (see above) or whenever red *adjika* salt is specified.

DRIED YELLOW MARIGOLD PETALS OR POWDER

Often called, to my ears rather sweetly, *kviteli kvevilli*, or "yellow flower," dried marigold (*Calendula officinalis*) is also frequently referred to as Imereti saffron – which is perhaps why I sometimes struggle with it as a flavoring, because it seems to have the faintest of aromas and not to be contributing much. But used in red *adjika* salt (see page 62), it adds a further earthiness, almost a mushroom-like umami if the accompanying spices are used in moderation. It's also valued for the color it brings to dishes.

Flavored salts & pastes

ADJIKA

The term *adjika* refers to a rather salty, aromatic chile condiment not too dissimilar to Tunisian harissa or Syrian *muhammara*. It can be as liquid as ketchup or it can come in the form of dry chile salt pellets. The best I have ever tried was from Samegrelo in western Georgia, but Abkhazia in the same region also prides itself on its own versions of this spicy flavor enhancer. In fact, it most probably originated from Abkhazia, as the name comes from Abkhazian word for "salt." It is the intensely flavored dry variety that I bring back with me to the UK in kilos, which no one really makes at home but instead buys ready-made at the market. However, having seen how it's made, I wanted to re-create it myself (see page 62).

The ingredients normally include red chile, garlic, blue fenugreek, and salt, although sometimes it can be very mild and contain more red bell peppers than chiles. There are also varieties where green chiles or mint are included (see page 25). Walnuts can also feature in *Abkhazi adjika*, or tomatoes in watered-down commercially produced versions in Russian food stores, which I wouldn't waste my money on.

SVANETI SALT

This is famous in Georgia and is made in a very similar way to the red *adjika* salt (see above) in Samegrelo. Besides salt, it contains raw garlic and a wide variety of spices including blue fenugreek and dill seeds.

Fruit & vegetables

ALYCHA PLUMS

Green, hard, and extremely sour when unripe, these plums make an exceptional addition to herby spring lamb stews. They can be preserved whole, or turned into a dry paste or fruit leather (see page 228).

BARBERRIES

Luckily Yotam Ottolenghi has already done some groundwork in introducing this beautiful wild berry to a wider audience. Barberries are not only used extensively in Middle Eastern cooking, but also in Georgian and Azerbaijani dishes. Sold as whole dried berries or sometimes in flakes, they bring a distinctive acidity to dishes, added to stews or stirred through fresh salads – as versatile as they are delicious. You can find dried barberries fairly easily in Middle Eastern shops and online, but if you ever get a chance to travel to Azerbaijan, Armenia, or Georgia in the summer, visit the Deserters' Market in Georgia's capital, Tbilisi, and keep an eye out for fresh, plump, juicy barberries from the mountainous region of Tusheti.

CHICKPEAS

If you use chickpeas, dried are always best. However, if time is of the essence, do try and source chickpeas in brine, which are sold in glass jars at good Italian delis. I think they have a superior flavor and texture. I've learnt this trick from Sabrina Ghayour, who really knows her chickpeas.

EKALA

From what I can gather, *ekala* is primarily an Imereti (a region in western Georgia) wild plant with the rather amusing botanical name of *Smelax excelsa*. It is a type of spinach, even though it's nothing like the iron-rich, leafy vegetable we are used to in the West. I'm an ingredient junky, constantly on the lookout for new and exciting items, so *ekala* immediately caught my eye at markets all over Georgia. It has spindly curly offshoots not unlike the tendrils of a grapevine. If you have ever tasted grapevine shoots, this has a similar, slightly sour flavor, but it's also a little musky and wild-tasting.

FRUIT LEATHER

Called *tklapi* in Georgia, *lavashak* in Armenian, and *lavashana* in Azerbaijani, fruit leathers are rife in the Caucasus, just as they are in Iran. Huge 5-gallon (20-liter) pots of fresh fruit juice or purée are balanced over some smoldering fruitwood logs, slowly bubbling and reducing into a thick syrup. Given the volume, it can take a day or two for it to reduce sufficiently. Then it is poured over a cotton sheet, spread into a thin layer, and when dry kept between sheets of paper all winter. Pieces of it are then given to kids as delicious natural treats. Sometimes these sour-fragrant sheets are soaked in water and then added to stews and soups to add a gorgeous fruity note. You can find them ready-made, but you can also (if you have a glut of superb fruit) follow my recipe and make your own *tklapi* (see page 216). And here you are not restricted to specific ingredients; just use the best local fruit available.

GREEN GARLIC

This is simply new-season, young garlic and luckily it is becoming more and more widely available with each spring.

WILD GARLIC

The people of Armenia, Georgia, Azerbaijan, and other Caucasian countries love wild herbs, and they collect and cook with hundreds of different varieties, which makes you realize how urbanized and removed from nature the rest of us are. But we don't have to be. Even if you live in an urban area, you may be able to track down and pick wild garlic easily.

JONJOLI

"Colchis bladdernut" is the unglamorous common name for *jonjoli* (accent on the first "o"), which sounds like wind chime crystals singing in the wind, whereas bladdernut sounds... let's forget about bladdernut. *Jonjoli* looks as beautiful as its Georgian name – a tall shrub with grape-like clusters of unopened white flower buds. Georgians pick them and pack them with salt into humongous jars, then leave them to ferment. No caper, which it is often likened to in flavor, comes even close in comparison. By way of a substitute, look for so-called acacia trees in your area, actually false acacia or black locust (*Robinia pseudoacacia*), as their unopened flowers, which appear in late spring, are sometimes used instead of *jonjoli* in Georgia (be careful not to use any leaves, as they are toxic). I have served *jonjoli* many times in London and beyond, and people go crazy for it. What is this strange, dangly, caper-like bud, they ask? *Jonjoli!* Sorry, I can't stop saying it – *jonjolijonjolijonjoli*...

PURSLANE

The wonderful sea purslane is to be found in the UK growing wild in wetlands by the sea. But in Georgia and other regions of the Caucasus (as well as Greece, Cyprus, Turkey, and other Mediterranean regions), it grows where no other plant will, pushing its meaty, salty, slightly tart leaves through gravel on the side of the road, popping up in people's neglected gardens, anywhere. It can be eaten raw, but I like to blanch it for just twenty seconds to mellow its flavor and make it more digestible. I am lucky enough to live on the porch of London's Turkish and

Cypriot heaven that is Green Lanes in North London, and my local greengrocer sells it in the summer. If there is no way you can get hold of sea purslane, don't despair. You can use some other beautiful greens such as Swiss chard or spring greens – their earthy tones will work equally well.

SORREL

Ahhh, sorrel. It is my favorite leaf. I grew up with it in Ukraine, and I encountered it again in the Caucasus. But common sorrel or garden sorrel (*Rumex acetosa*) is also native to the British Isles and to be found throughout Europe and in parts of North America, yet it's an often forgotten or at least underrated leaf. I really hope that we can all start a sorrel revolution and make it widely available. It is so easy to grow, tastes like a lemony dream, and is beautiful added to broths or used fresh in salads.

TKEMALI

Alycha plums, either in their green unripe state or ripe yellow and red, are used to make one of the most important condiments in Georgia, *tkemali* sauce. I don't know if Caucasian cooking could continue if *tkemali* suddenly disappeared; it's almost sacred. Some cook it for a while, resulting in thick, spicy, garlicky purée, but it's the fresher, barely cooked version that I love the most. It is served with everything – grilled meat, shallow-fried river trout, vegetables. Beet cooked in *tkemali* was for me a revelation bordering on an epiphany. Beet and plums – but of course! Earthy, firm, and sweet beet paired with slightly caustic and juicy plum: a Burton and Taylor marriage in its intensity and call for repetition (see page 23 for a recipe).

UNREFINED SUNFLOWER OIL

I mentioned this beautiful ingredient in my debut book *Mamushka*, and I feel I have to mention it again, as Georgians, like their Ukrainian sisters and brothers, adore this oil. Nothing to do with the highly processed sunflower oil we are used to in the West – it is deep golden in color and nutty in flavor. Imagine toasting a load of sunflower seeds and then squashing them over your salad – this is what it will taste like. And it is used (raw, never cooked) extensively – over salads, over fermented vegetables, always over *jonjoli* (see opposite) and thinly sliced red onions. It is also served with a light sprinkling of red pepper flakes and sea salt for bread to be dipped into, just like Italians do with superb olive oils.

Herbs

OMBALO

Imagine marjoram and mint making love on some swampy marshes and bearing a wild herb child as a result. This is what *ombalo* (*Mentha pulegium*, also commonly known as pennyroyal) tastes like to me. It sings and makes your head spin when you taste it in a sauce or sprinkled over some incredible tomatoes. If you can't source it, spearmint mixed with marjoram is closest in flavor, but if that is also difficult to find fresh, use a little bit of good-quality dried mint in your sauce.

PURPLE BASIL

Azerbaijanis call this *reikhan*, a suitably regal-sounding word. It is a rather flamboyant king of herbs in my opinion. Sweet, with a slight aniseed kick, he is far superior to his green brother. Laid out among other herbs on the table as part of a standard feast accompaniment to other dishes (just pick a sprig and eat it all, including the stalk) or sprinkled into a saffron-hued *dyushbara* broth (see page 111), it adds a curious layer to most dishes. It also loves the company of other soft herbs – chop it up and mix with a little tarragon and mint, lots of cilantro, and a handful of dill, then add to your butter-roasted chicken at the end of cooking. The flavor will blow your socks off.

SUMMER SAVORY

In the eastern Mediterranean and in Georgia, a few wild plants of the mint family are known by the same name, so it took me some time to figure out what it was that Georgians called *kondari*. Is it oregano, wild mint, wild thyme, or mountain savory? It turns out that wild winter savory (*Satureja montana*) and summer savory (*Satureja hortensis*) are the plants that Georgians call *kondari* and use extensively in cooking. A Middle Eastern name for it seems to be *za'atar*, although this is also the name given to Syrian oregano (*Origanum syriacum*) as well the *za'atar* spice mix, just to add to the confusion! Summer savory has a more pronounced flavor than winter savory, and this is the one they use most.

Wild things

In the mountains of Georgia you can forage for and eat wild sorrel leaves, bilberry leaves, and berries and wild strawberries and raspberries, which taste about five times more intense and sweet than the cultivated varieties. Wild walnuts are smaller but again more pronounced in flavor. How can all of these ingredients not be, as they grow alongside each other, drinking mountain spring water and influencing each other's flavors? Some plants I've encountered in Svaneti, a gorgeous northwestern province of Georgia, I have never seen anywhere else – the thorny *kotzakhuri* shrub with edible leaves, *letsiri* stalks, barberry leaves. Imereti mushrooms were the best I have ever eaten in my whole life, and I've sampled some spectacular mushrooms. If you ever get the chance to drive from Tbilisi in the direction of western Georgia and it has been raining, shout and stop the car if you spot roadside vendors. They are foragers and they might have something that Georgians call *mchadi* mushroom (*mchadi* being a local dense corn flatbread). The mushrooms are small, very dark in color, and very dense. Even when cooked, they retain an almost raw-like, crisp texture. The flavor is…almost indescribable. The closest I came in comparison was sucking the juices out of a red Spanish prawn's head, so imagine that but in a mushroom context.

Dairy

BUTTER

I tried buffalo butter in Azerbaijani Qebele region that made me want to stuff it in my pocket and eat it like cheese later in the car. I've encountered a similar product in Georgia, homemade by many a woman in the mountains. Butter can be much more than what we are used to. One of the reasons why milk and all the things that come from it, such as cheese and butter, are so incredibly good in the Caucasus is because of where the cows, buffaloes, goats, and sheep roam and what they eat. Seeing cows dexterously picking rosehips with their lips, as well as a thousand other wild-growing plants, puts it all into perspective. Even though I have not encountered buffalo butter in the UK, I know a person who makes the most incredible cultured Jersey butter. Young Grant Harrington (he is literally in his early twenties!) is currently making some of the most spectacular fermented butter in the country. Of course, you can use any good-quality commercial butter.

CHEESE

They make outstanding cheese in the Caucasus. So special, so flavorsome, so widely available but sadly not so in the West. I despaired writing some of these recipes. How on earth can they translate to another context if the cheese doesn't taste of wild meadows consumed by tiny, agile Caucasian cows? There is, however, a way forward. If you don't get to travel to Georgia or Armenia and sample the real thing, check out your local farms and small-scale producers for artisanal, unpasteurized cheeses. They may not be made using the same techniques, and they will no doubt be made from the milk of massive dairy cows rather than tiny Georgian cows, but it is absolutely possible to find the right stuff. If you care about your food and quality produce and the people who put a lot of time and effort into creating it, you will be able to come very close to replicating the flavors that knocked my socks off in dreamy Caucasia. If all else fails and you are a cheese-making enthusiast, check out the fresh cheese and *suluguni* recipes (see pages 107 and 108) and make your own!

MATSONI, MAZOON & KATYK

These are basically homemade yogurts that use a Caspian strain of bacteria to make a starter called *deda* in Georgian, which translates as "mother." Once you've made this kind of yogurt at home, you won't be able to look at supermarket yogurt in the same way again, as the flavor and texture differ significantly from what we are used to commercially, and it is full of healthy bacteria. You will need to find proper milk, by which I mean raw milk. Some say that it's OK to use non-homogenized milk, but I think raw is actually what is needed here. You may also need to source some yogurt bacteria.

In the ancient western Georgian Samegrelo dialect (some say language), *bzha* means "milk," but it also means "sun," which must make it the most gorgeous homonym in linguistic history. "Darling, pour some sun into my tea, would you?" I wish English was as effortlessly poetic sometimes. But it makes sense. This is how holy dairy products are considered to be, not only in Georgia but also in the whole of the Caucasus. Picture small agile cows, the size of a large goat, hopping around the mountains, munching on rosehips, berries, flowers, and a cornucopia of wild herbs. They are so tiny and muscular that they produce half the volume of milk that a dairy cow provides. But just imagine the unique flavor of that milk – it is very nutritious and fatty, and it tastes of the wild mountainous terrain.

Meat

KURDYUK FAT

This is fat from the rump of a special fat-rumped (or fat-tailed) breed of sheep found in Azerbaijan and Central Asia that look like they have massive humps on their bums. This fat is DELICIOUS. It's firm in texture and doesn't melt away but crisps up when cooked. In Central Asia they have a ceremonial dish where they cook the whole rump with the fat intact until super crispy, and then they slice and eat it. A Thai friend of mine who has tried it now dreams of having it with some spicy *nahm jim* sauce, which I can relate to. I doubt if you will be able to find *kurdyuk* fat anywhere in the West. Some Turkish halal butchers may have something similar, but unfortunately it may never be as flavorsome as what you would find in the Caucasus and Central Asia. So go to your butcher and ask him to give you trimmings from the best-fed, tastiest lamb they have, such as salt-marsh lamb – it will add an incredible flavor. We have learnt to use pig's fat in the Ukraine in a similar way; for instance, when we make *manty*, or pork dumplings, we use good pork and mix it with a little lightly cured pork fat that we call *salo*. Good Italian *lardo* (in chunks rather than thinly sliced) will also do the trick.

Wine

Here I am talking exclusively about the Georgian natural-wine revolution. The ancient winemaking traditions of Georgia, with its hundreds of endemic grape varieties, had been quashed by the industrialist behemoth that was the Soviet Union. Land was seized, only commercially viable grape varieties planted, and thousand-year-old techniques abandoned. Giant Georgian clay fermentation pots called *qvevri* and the masters that made them almost disappeared. And then, circa 2006, a miracle happened. The near-vanished art was rediscovered by prominent French winemakers, and then picked up by the descendants of traditional Georgian winemakers all over the country. And they started making wine, the real deal, using pre-industrialized, naturally fermented grape juices that taste like honeysuckle, farmyard, and dried apricots. These are not easy-drinking wines that you would sup in a bar. These are wines that really shine when paired with delicious foods, even with foods that are generally considered hard to match with wine.

Part of the reason for this is because many of the red wines are made using a white-grape method involving very little skin contact (maceration time) and resulting in light-bodied fresh reds. And white wine grapes are allowed to ferment along with their stalks and skins, like reds normally would be, and left together for nine months in the *qvevri* (or, as Georgians say, left with their *deda*, or mother), the natural "womb" handcrafted from local slate and clay, buried into the Earth's belly, producing the most spectacular orange wines known to humanity.

These wines are a far cry from the bland aperitif wines made on a terrifyingly industrial scale. They are not even comparable to expensive commercially produced wines laden with sulfur. They are alive, like any fermented produce should be; they live and they change. The old grapevines are allowed to grow naturally in their wild surroundings, the true "terroir," among wild summer savory and clover, with minimum human intervention. As the doyenne of wine writing, Alice Feiring, observed, "... how a thinking person could actually believe agriculture was irrelevant to flavor... people who were committed to organic produce forgot that grapes that made wine were produce as well. ... It was commonplace to eat organic yet drink conventional." And I agree with her. If these thoughts resonate with you, or if you are simply curious, I highly recommend her book *For the Love of Wine*.

Since some of these wines have made it onto the wine lists of Yotam Ottolenghi's restaurants, they definitely deserve a place on your wine rack at home. And besides, I have personally never had a hangover from drinking them; slow brain, sure, but not that throbbing physical pain. But if instead you decide to shun this natural-wine ode and drink the rubbish from your corner shop, turn to page 144 and the chapter entitled "Pain, be gone!" for some effective remedies.

Sources

SPICES & CONDIMENTS
The suppliers below stock ingredients such as *khmeli-suneli*, blue fenugreek, *tkemali*, and other unusual ingredients.

Bazaar Spices
www.bazaarspices.com

Caucasian Spice Box
www.caucasians.co.uk

English Saffron
www.englishsaffron.co.uk

Georgian Gourmet
www.georgiangourmet.com

Kalustyan's
www.kalustyans.com

Persepolis
www.foratasteofpersia.co.uk

Seasoned Pioneers
www.seasonedpioneers.com

Spicely Organics
www.spicely.com

World Spice Merchants
www.worldspice.com

CHEESE
These shops carry a range of international cheeses, including raclette and Ogleshield.

Murray's Cheese
www.murrayscheese.com

The Cheese Store of Beverly Hills
www.cheesestorebh.com

Zingerman's
www.zingermans.com

MEAT
Find good-quality meat, as well as ethically produced meat, from these suppliers.

44 Farms
www.44farms.com

D'Artagnan
www.dartagnan.com

Meat the Butchers
www.meatthebutchers.com

Organic Prairie
www.organicprairie.com

GEORGIAN WINE
Natural Georgian Wine
www.lescaves.co.uk

GUESTHOUSES IN GEORGIA
Fangani Family Guest House
Vealge Becho (near Mazeri)
Svaneti, Georgia
Tel: +995 598 42 61 92
Email: inu.fangani@gmail.com

Guest House Ketino Sujashvili
Qvemo Gergeti Str.22
4700 Kazbegi, Georgia
Tel: +995 571 03 24 39
Email: ketinosujashvili@mail.ru

Marina Nariashvili
Guest House Edemi
Rustaveli Street 105a
Akhaltsikhe, Georgia
Tel: +995 599 18 51 59
Email: 105edemi@gmail.com

RESTAURANTS IN GEORGIA
Azarphesha
2, Pavle Ingorokva St.
Tbilisi, Georgia
Tel : +995 322 98 23 46
E-mail: info@azarphesha.com
Wine restaurant

Poliphonia
23, Amaghleba St.
Tbilisi, Georgia
Tel : +995 557 63 71 43

Vino Underground
15, Galaktion Tabidze St.
Tbilisi, Georgia
www.vinounderground.ge
Wine bar

Pheasant's Tears
18, Baratashvili St.
Sighnaghi, Georgia
www.pheasantstears.com
Wine restaurant

Barbarestan
D. Aghmashenebeli Ave.
132, Tbilisi 0112, Georgia
Tel: +995 322 94 37 79

Culinarium
1 Mikheil Lermontovi St.
Tbilisi, Georgia
Tel : +995 32 2 43 01 03
Email: info@culinarium.ge
(open Thursday–Sunday, reservations only)

Khasheria
23, Abano St.
Tbilisi, Georgia
Tel: +995 322 72 11 57

Café Littera
13 Ivane Machabeli St.
Tbilisi 0105, Georgia
Tel: +995 595 03 11 12

Index

Bold pagination indicates main recipe

Author's acknowledgments

So many kind people have been involved in making this book possible – if I fail to mention someone, please forgive me. And, reader, forgive the soppiness that follows, I cannot help it.

Thank you, Octopus, the best cookbook publisher in the world, and to Stephanie Jackson, who has given me this opportunity and more. Thank you for letting me keep my voice and my vision; I know how lucky I am – not a lot of authors get this.

Sybella, you are the most skilled editor I have ever met. When I read the edited text, it is hard to pinpoint what you have done, but I know you have done something, giving my ramblings such a smooth flow. Thank you for your gentle patience and encouragement.

Thank you to Denise Bates, Caroline Brown, Kevin Hawkins, and everyone at Octopus who has helped make *Mamushka* such an immense success.

Miranda Harvey and Juliette Norsworthy – thank you for creating such a timeless, laconic design, and for including so much of my writing without its looking overbearing.

Grace, once again, thank you for transferring my vision into the cover – it's another classic.

Cara O'Sullivan, thank you for your beautiful hand-cut art of a map – it is now hanging, framed, in my kitchen. You are an amazing talent.

Thank you, Ariella and Aoife, for being the coolest, sweetest agents one can hope for. I am so chuffed I have not let you down.

Thank you, Elena Heatherwick, for giving our project so much more than was ever expected. For sacrificing time with your son and for giving it your all. As my brother Sasha said, "Elena photographs souls." You really do – souls of people, souls of landscapes, and your food photography is unique and timeless. This book is also yours, it would not be the same without you. I love you, you are my kindred spirit.

I would like to thank my Aunt Nina Grebenyuk, half-Armenian, half-Ukrainian, who inspired me with her stories of her childhood in Karabakh. Hours of our conversations have now traveled from the dictaphone onto these pages, giving them so much depth, color, and meaning.

A special thank you goes to Keti and Zezva Maghlakelidze of Caucasian Spice Box, who were the first link in the spontaneous chain of people who have followed and selflessly helped me research the area in the most natural way possible. Keti, thank you for all your help, you define Caucasian hospitality without my ever having visited your house!

Thank you also to Nino Baratashvili, you have inspired the "*dedakatsi*" essay and beyond. Also your mum and grandmother's recipes are some of the most cherished – I want you to know that.

Thank you to John Wurderman and Ketivan Mindorashvili for all the stories, thoughts, and feasts and for connecting me with the most incredible people. Gia and Tina Rokashvili, thank you for welcoming us at Pheasant's Tears and for sharing your time, knowledge, and outstanding recipes. Who needs a Michelin star when one can eat food like yours, Gia?

So many precious recipes in this book would be missing had it not been for Ketino Sujashvili, Marina Nariashvili, Galina and family, Zhuzhuna and Anna, Tea Chitadze. Also my sweet adoptive Georgian mother Ia Kerzala – you are amazing – thank you for giving me your recipes and also a crash course on Somegrelo dialect and all things etymological.

The Fangani family: Tina, Lasha, Amiran – you are some of the kindest, warmest people I have ever met. I will never forget how you cared for us in your guesthouse with that medieval chapel hanging around so casually in your back garden! You live in one of the most beautiful places in the world.

Another special thanks to one of my now dearest friends, Ének Peterson, for your guidance; editing and contributing to my essay about wine; for your kindness; the amazing dishes you created when we were cooking together; and for endless inspiration. You are the future, and an immense natural talent – I hope the people in Georgia see it and you get to cook just the way you cook at Vino Underground.

Thank you to the Akobidze family for giving us your beautiful home in Tbilisi when you did not even know us, during such a sad and difficult time for you all. I will never forget your kindness.

Thank you to all the natural-wine makers, and their wives and mothers, for welcoming us and sharing the beautiful wines and recipes. I am so proud to know you, Nestan and Ramaz Nikoladze, and of course sweet Tsegunya, with your immense energy.

Thank you for your time and inspiration, Tamaz Dundua, Irakli Cholobargia, Anastasia Lundqvist, Tekuna Gachechiladze. Thank you to all the kids from Artana for providing sanctuary and keeping me sane when I thought I was on the brink of physical and mental exhaustion (my sweet friends Tengo, Ketino and Kakha Berishvili, Tamuna, Ramazik, Sandro – thank you).

Thank you to our guides Shota Lagazidze (I too love vegetables, especially in spring) and to Akaki for taking us all around Georgia and for deep conversations, light laughter, and some excellent Georgian tunes.

Thank you, Anya Von Bremzen, for connecting me with Zulfiya and Rufat Kazimov, who are now like family to us. Zulya, I thought that Georgians could not be beaten in their hospitality, but you have matched them and more. Thank you for letting us meet your family in Lankaran, that was a truly special time. I will come back and bring the book for Mehriban, Nazilya, Shafak, and Imran.

Farkhad Ashurbeyli and the gang, thank you for the incredible off-roading recipe hunt trips. I will never forget our adventures.

Thank you to all the brilliant recipe testers and friends: Caroline Parry (and also for your support, as always), Sarah Eden, Sara Haider, Alissa Timoshkina, Mari Volkosh, Dara Sutin, Chris Bailey, and John Holland, Sara Haider, Concepta Cassar, Thomas Eagle, Richard Snapes and Eve Hemingway, Nico Ghiraldo.

A special mention goes to Carl and Deb Legge (of Permaculture Kitchen) – thank you for developing all the cheese-making recipes, for explaining the science behind it, and for testing them so expertly.

Allan Jenkins, thank you for giving me a kick when I needed one.

Thank you to all the amazing assistants: Brian Gamble, Harry Sergeant, and others for supporting us and making things so much easier.

Diana Henry, thank you for your ongoing support – I want to be like you when I grow up.

Nigella Lawson, Jamie Oliver – thank you both, what an honor to have your words of support.

Alice Feiring, thank you for your books – your knowledge of Georgia and natural wines is inspirational.

To our mums, Olga and Liliana, for taking care of our small boys while we were away shooting for long periods of time. Single parenting is not easy, and we couldn't have done it without you. Tim Catley, thank you also for being such an amazing grandma to Sasha.

To my brother Aleksandr – please come back, we miss you painfully. And to my dad, Petro, *dyakuyu tato* for all your hard work and for teaching me that kindness is the most important thing in the world.

Sasha, my son, I am sorry I am away so much, this is all for you, always. I hope you will be proud of your mum. Joe Woodhouse, thank you for finding me when I'd lost all hope, for changing my life, inspiring me, and making me love. I now feel recharged and complete and utterly happy.